THE EFFECTIVE PRESENTATION

THE ONCOME PRESENTATION

THE EFFECTIVE PRESENTATION

Talk Your Way to Success

Asha Kaul

Response Books
A division of Sage Publications
New Delhi/Thousand Oaks/London

First published in 2005 by

Response Books
A division of Sage Publications India Pvt Ltd
B-42, Panchsheel Enclave
New Delhi 110 017

Sage Publications Inc	**Sage Publications Ltd**
2455 Teller Road	1 Oliver's Yard
Thousand Oaks	55 City Road
California 91320	London EC1Y 1SP

Published by Tejeshwar Singh for Response Books, typeset in Souvenir 10.5/13 pts. by Innovative Processors, New Delhi, and printed at Chaman Enterprises, New Delhi.

Library of Congress Cataloging-in-Publication Data

Kaul, Asha.
    The effective presentation : talk your way to success/Asha Kaul.
        p. cm.
    1. Business presentations. 2. Visual communication. 3. Oral communication. I. Title.
HF5718.22.K38 2005   658.4′52—dc22   2005019717

ISBN: 0–7619–3413–8 (US Pb)   81–7829–569–5 (India Pb)

Production Team: Gargi Dasgupta, R.A.M. Brown and
                Santosh Rawat

To
My Mother and Father

Thanks for always being there

Contents

Contents

Preface

The Effective Presentation: Talk Your Way to Success is a response to the growing needs of the corporate and academic world to make effective presentations. My assumption in the book is that the technique for success lies in the ability to master the art of making effective presentations. Beginning with this premise I have attempted to provide the reader with elementary and technical know-how of making presentations that will have long lasting impact. This text is a result of teaching and training experience at various academic institutes and business houses. The examples thus are drawn from the real world and case studies designed specifically for the purpose of developing and enhancing presentation skills. *The Effective Presentation: Talk Your Way to Success* will help readers understand the importance of sound presentations and help them to prepare and deliver ideas effectively.

I have tried to use a conversational and user friendly style for the text. *The Effective Presentation: Talk Your Way to Success* walks the readers through the process of preparing and delivering effective presentations. Methods of conducting research, analysis of audience expectations, organization of ideas, creation of visual aids and finally the process of presentation are discussed. Designed for corporates, teachers and students alike the book proceeds with multiple examples that will aid the reader in self assessment and enhancement of skills.

PEDAGOGY

1. Objectives: Learning objectives at the beginning of every chapter make the reading easy and focused. All sections within chapters commence with an objective which helps the reader to understand the goal of the section which is linked to the overall objective of the chapter. Stated learning objectives at all levels in the book are brief and measurable.

2. Rules: A set of Ten Commandments in each chapter makes it easy for the reader to grasp the concepts at a glance and check for coherence and clarity in the preparation and presentation stage.

3. Checklists: Each chapter in the book is provided with a checklist to help readers proceed through the text at a fast pace.

4. Visuals: Exhibits and tables simplify the learning process and add to the visual appeal of the text.

5. Summary: Summary highlights and reiterates the key points discussed in the chapter.

STRUCTURE OF THE BOOK

Chapter I: Introduction. Chapter I spells out the need for the book, the advantages to be gained from a thorough study of the techniques. The chapter proceeds to detail the need for making presentations, the benefits accruing from a successful adoption of techniques. The different types of presentations, informative and persuasive and their uses are exemplified. Differences between planned and unplanned speeches are also detailed.

Chapter II: Planning a Presentation. Chapter II reiterates the need for structuring ideas and thoughts before presenting them before a large or small gathering. The need, the necessity for planning and the process are meticulously detailed. Minute details are exemplified and examples are used to gently lead the reader to a final conclusion.

Chapter III: Structuring a Presentation. Chapter III maintains emphasis on discussing techniques for structuring a persuasive and informative presentation. Step by step techniques for improving the quality of presentations are discussed and strategies presented for making a presentation appealing and captivating.

Chapter IV: Creating Visual Aids (VAs). The uses of visual aids to improve the quality of presentations are discussed in this chapter. The choice of visual aids, criteria for selection design and development which simplify and clarify the procedure and process are detailed.

Chapter V: Delivering a Presentation: While Chapters II, III, and IV discuss behind the screen activities, Chapter V leads the reader front-stage, ready and well-equipped to talk and present before a gathering. The importance of good voice articulation and positive body language and their impact on the audience are discussed. Strategies for bringing about a change if needed are also discussed in detail.

Chapter VI: Situational Presentation: Chapter VI provides certain situations, which can be appropriately used by the reader to practice. It is a chapter which attempts to get the reader into the "think on your feet" mode. Most of the strategies learned in Chapters I–III and V can be applied in these situations. I have deliberately left out Chapter IV as it discusses design of visual aids which in these impromptu situations is not possible.

Acknowledgements

My parents, Vimla and Gyan Nath Kaul have always been a constant moral support to me in all my endeavours. I am and will always remain indebted to them for their encouragement. My sincere thanks are also due to my mother–in–law, Dr Kamal Kumari Kaul for her silent support.

The book is a product of concerted effort of my Trainee Academic Associates Esha Patnaik, Mamta Mohanty and Vaibhavi Kulkarni. A heartfelt thanks to the three of you … without your unstinting support to my untimely demands the book would never have been written. Thanks to Professor Hiromitsu Hayashida, Chuo University, Japan for providing an intellectually stimulating environment.

I would like to extend my gratitude to Chapal Mehra, Managing Editor, Response Books, who patiently tolerated my multiple extensions for submission of draft. Thank you, Leela Kirloskar, Consulting Editor, Response Books, for patiently going through the draft and making valuable and useful suggestions.

Last but not the least, thanks to Harsh, Anand and Rohini for the entertaining interludes and intermissions, a must for every author!

List of Tables

List of Figures

List of Figures

List of Exhibits

Chapter 1

Introduction

Nothing is so unbelievable that oratory cannot make it acceptable.

—Marcus Tullius Cicero
Roman Statesman

One machine can do the work of fifty ordinary men. No machine can do the work of one extraordinary man.

—Elbert Hubbard

OBJECTIVES

- ❑ Identify the need for a book on presentation skills
- ❑ Learn about the benefits of using the book
- ❑ Zero in on the appropriate methodology of application of concepts
- ❑ Learn the need for a presentation
- ❑ Identify the different types and forms of presentations

Key Words	
Direct reporting	Presentations
Informative presentations	Planned presentations
Large group presentation	Public speaking
Persuasive presentations	Unplanned presentations
	Small group presentations

The single most important aspect of communication is the ability to speak, to talk and to present convincingly to the audience. The growing needs of all organizations and institutions spell the necessity of sharing ideas, thoughts and concepts. The only method through which this can be achieved is by communicating and presenting your ideas.

Some questions that come to the mind are: What is the need or the purpose of making presentations? Why should we present our ideas?

Simply stated, the purpose and need of making a presentation is to either tune team and group members to your manner of thinking or, to provide information. The objective of the presentation then is to get your message across in a fashion in which it is understood and remembered.

The advantages of making a presentation are many. This form of communication:

- ❑ Helps in projection of the presenter
- ❑ Provides a platform for sharing ideas
- ❑ Facilitates learning
- ❑ Aids in building confidence

To make the most of this book and to enhance the much required skill of making presentations, let us take a close look at who should be the target audience and what is the benefit/value add that can be derived from this book.

WHO SHOULD USE THIS BOOK?

Let us look at a few scenarios:

1. Amit is a student who has just completed an interesting project. The teacher asks him to present the findings of his research to a class of 40 graduate students. Amit is ready and raring to go! But somewhere in the corner of his heart he is a little concerned and apprehensive. Will he be able to get his message across? Will the authenticity and the validity of his work come through in his presentation? Will he be able to present the work in a convincing way?

2. Meenakshi has been a teacher for the last five years. She has sound technical knowledge, has presented many papers at international conferences, and has many books to her credit. However, when it comes to teaching, she is not able to make an impact in the classroom. Some students feel there is an information overload, others feel that her sessions are not focused and therefore, boring and monotonous. As a result, a few of the students sleep in her class, while others play naughts and crosses. Meenakshi is worried and concerned. How should she proceed? What will make her presentations to the students interesting?

3. Vijay is a busy, high-flying executive who has moved up the ladder of success by sheer dint of hard work and sleepless nights. His competency level and skill set is probably the best in the organization. What more does he need to reach the top position in the organization? Will ambition and lots of hard work

suffice? What is the extra plus he needs to make him succeed?

Not surprisingly, the answer to all the questions presented in the three scenarios above is the same— good communication and still better communication—the guru mantra for success.

You may wonder why communication skills are so important? How will these help you to achieve that much coveted position in the academia or the organization? The answer is not hard to find—honing communication skills will help in better understanding your audience, and formulating a message that they can easily relate to.

To further elaborate, all tasks are almost always completed in teams. It is rare that you are the only student/ member working on a project. Interaction, exchange between and among team members is common. Achieving success in these interactions is the job of the communicator who must possess the capability to convince and persuade the audience, provide information on issues related to the topic at hand and listen accurately and astutely to the comments of the group members.

Time constraints, peer pressures, differences in opinion, and politics at work collectively bog you down. The result—sham presentations and meetings, with members either not willing to contribute or ready to pick up the sword.

Let us try and change the scenario. Despite time and peer pressures, you have made an attempt to understand the various opinions of the audience, acknowledged their attempts and tried to amalgamate the viewpoints and present a noveau picture. The result—greater participation, more ideas, higher interest and better solutions.

How did you manage this change in situation? By your abilities as an ace communicator! An important part of communication is the ability to understand the needs/ expectations of the audience in the group, listen to their ideas, weave them in self generated concepts and PRESENT/TALK.

Talking or presenting successfully is one sure way of scaling great heights. The secrets are not many nor are they hard to acquire. A scientific and objective understanding of the skill helps in acquiring, polishing and honing already existing capabilities.

WHAT'S IN THIS BOOK?

This book is a repertoire of all the techniques and strategies essential for making a presentation. All of us at some time or the other have been asked to make presentations. Some have been hailed as successful and great presenters, while others have not been so successful. Let us for a moment introspect and truthfully answer the questions:

'Was I successful?'

'If yes, do I want to improve still further or am I content with my success?'

'If no, what can I do to be successful in future presentations?'

Additionally, let us ask ourselves some more questions:

'Can I rise to great heights by acquiring/honing presentation skills?'

'Can I teach these skills to my subordinates/students?'

'Can making presentations be taught or learned?'

If your answer to any one of these questions or for all of them is yes, this book is a must read.

The book deals with almost all the known strategies for making impressive and convincing presentations. The essentials for any presentation, be it to a small or large group, be it to members in the organization or the academia, are listed and illustrated in a succinct manner.

Voice articulation, body language, design of content and visuals are all explained and illustrations provided wherever necessary. Explanations and illustrations together with the listed points will aid readers to:

❑ Assess their own capabilities
❑ Analyse strategies used
❑ Apply concepts; and
❑ Witness the result

HOW TO USE AND BENEFIT FROM THIS BOOK?

This book is written on the simple principles of application. It proceeds by providing illustrations and examples, analysis, solutions and suggestions. The solutions provided are not final or ultimate. They are guidelines which will help every presenter take stock of self-presentation capabilities, proceed and develop in a direction most suited to the occasion and the situation.

Let me exemplify with the help of an illustration...

One of the strategies for use of body language, referred to in the book, cautions the presenter on excessive movements and use of hands. However, you would have noticed some very successful presenters sit on the table, roll up their sleeves and talk casually to the audience, creating a mind-boggling effect. These presenters, you can question, have violated all principles of body language and are still good, even excellent. Why then must principles and norms for making presentations be studied?

Are these principles relevant? What is their merit in the current corporate/academic/other scenarios?

The relevance and applicability of these principles becomes evident when you begin a candid assessment of yourself. Have you been able to acquire a style of presentation for which you are recognized, acknowledged and appreciated? Even if you have, some basic, guiding principles are needed which will help you develop a style which is typically representative of you. And if you haven't, the reasons for adhering to principles and norms are self explanatory.

Additionally, in each presenter there are strengths and areas for improvement. This book attempts to help you strengthen skills you possess and focus on areas for improvement. Checklists at the end of each chapter encapsulate the learning and aid in quick application of the concepts. Case studies, where necessary, are provided and worked on. They can be used as a starting point from which you can build and move confidently in your area of expertise and domain knowledge.

In other words, while domain knowledge is essential, competency to deliver this knowledge is equally important. This book helps you in translating your thoughts and concepts in a fashion which will be accepted and highly appreciated by the audience.

So far we have been discussing the relevance of presentations and their high import value. But ...

WHAT ARE PRESENTATIONS?

Presentations are ideas, concepts or issues that are talked about or shared with a group of people or an audience. It is immaterial whether the group size is small or large. What is important is that the presenter is convincing and is able to capture and hold the attention of the audience.

Presentations are developed with the explicit purpose of conveying a message to an audience. The mode can be formal or informal, the audience internal or external, and the medium dependent on the availability of the equipment or devices at the venue.

There has been considerable debate in the academia on the use/abuse of equipments as visual aids for presentations. One school of thought believes that these modern techniques negate the position and role of the presenter, whereas the other school is of the firm opinion that a presentation is enhanced with visual aids.

More important than following any school blindly, is your conviction—what will help you improve the quality of your presentation? You may decide to follow the dictates of one school for a particular style of presentation and the rules of another school for a different set of presentations. The guiding criterion in both must always be the same: to achieve thumping success!!

WHY MAKE PRESENTATIONS?

With the advent of technology, the first question that comes to mind is why make presentations at all? Everything that you need to communicate can be easily transmitted through emails or communicated via the telephone or tele- or video conferences.

Emails, while a good substitute for written communication, i.e., letters, can never replace oral communication. For instance, the contact with the presenter, the exchange of ideas in the course of the interaction, the immediate response, and instant clarifications are not possible through an email. Nor can telephonic talks replace presentations as the exchange is always one-to-one and the advantages of contact with the presenter are missing.

It is a fact that tele- and video conferences are gradually replacing traditional modes of presentations in which the speaker stands on the stage or a podium in front of the audience and delivers the speech. Between the two, video conferences are a more apt description of what presentations must entail. But as the name of this medium of communication suggests, it is a mode of discussion, of a 'conference', and hence, does not fall within the purview of a presentation. You may be asked to make a presentation to global clients using the medium of video conferencing. As the audience is able to view and hear the presenter, the techniques used in traditional methods of making presentations will also be applicable in this case.

In tele-conferences there is no direct contact with the presenter. You can only hear but not see the presenter. This medium is well suited for discussions, interviews and brief chats but definitely not presentations. An interesting example has been cited by many executives. Occasionally, the communicator gets long-winded and boring and the audience is not in a position to disconnect because of hierarchical constraints. So, they put the equipment on the mute mode and continue with their work! Advantage: kill two birds with one stone.

With the increase of interdisciplinary and cross-functional work and coordination between groups and teams, the necessity of making presentations to a diverse group of people is the call/need of the hour. One has to repeatedly drive home a viewpoint for other people to appreciate/acknowledge/comment on the existing structure and nature of work. The best bet is to make an oral presentation to a group where the multiplicity of ideas generated by a diverse group enriches the conceptual development.

The more presentations you make, the higher is the contact and the greater are the chances of collaboration, networking, sharing of ideas and views.

WHAT ARE GOOD AND BAD PRESENTATIONS?

At the time of planning/structuring or making a presentation, there is only one concern in the mind of the presenter: THE PRESENTATION SHOULD BE A SUCCESS! When all strive towards achieving success how then does it happen that some presentations are successful/or good and some unsuccessful/or bad? What are the defining parameters? Who decides on the success or failure of the presentation?

All presentations are geared towards the audience. If the audience is able to sense value in the presentation, full credit is given but if it is unable to identify any merit in the talk, the presenter and structure of the presentation is shunned.

Merely loading the audience with content does not lead to success in the presentation. The content has to be structured and formulated according to the needs, the expectations and the educational level of the audience. For example, a presentation to students on gender diversity is going to be very different from one made to corporate employees.

The same presentation cannot be used at both places. While the basic content remains the same, there will be variations in terms of examples, structuring of content, voice modulations, etc. With a change in audience the presentation will also undergo a change. What may be considered good by one group may not necessarily be considered good by another group with an almost similar profile. The confidence in the presenter, the belief in the self and the topic can be additional factors that lead to the success or failure of the presentation.

A good presentation then, is one in which the content and its design appeals to the audience; a bad presentation, one in which the content is not in tune with the expectations and needs of the audience.

DIFFERENCE BETWEEN PUBLIC SPEAKING AND PRESENTATIONS

Many people associate presentations with public speaking and often use them as synonyms. To speak of the two in the same breath is to a certain extent acceptable but to use the two sciences/skills synonymously is fallacious.

Public speaking and presentations both require oratory skills. The semblance between them ends at this point. Let us raise a few queries and analyse these two forms of orations.

Have you ever heard a national or an international political leader make a speech? Do you remember participating in a debate in school or college, or listening to one in which there was a fiery exchange of ideas with issues and concepts being volleyed back and forth? Contrast it with a presentation in either the corporate world or the academia. Can a presentation made by an HR manager, for example, to the finance department of the organization, be used to address a large gathering of say, 50 people? Or a public speech made by a political leader be used in the corporate setting? Can you identify similarities or dissimilarities between the two?

Yes and no! The similarities begin and end at the level of the passion and the energy deployed in both situations. But nothing beyond that! Definitely not the words, nor the gesticulation! Major reason for the dissimilarities lies in the objective of the two forms of orations. In a public speech, the appeal is more to the heart than to the intellect and in a presentation, the plea is to the intellect.

Let us take an example in which the political leader is making a speech to the audience before the elections. There are probably thousands of people in the gathering waiting to hear the speech. The leader must deliver the presentation in such a way that it has mass appeal and can be understood by all and sundry. If the leader merely adheres to the presentation of a report on the achievements of the party, chances are high that the masses will not be able to comprehend his message and the election will be lost.

The presenter must cater to the different interest groups in the audience. For instance, out of the multiple interest groups, one group may be impressed by the personal achievements of the leader or those of the party, another by the speech intonations, the third by the emotional appeal and a fourth by the stories and anecdotes— the 'masala' in the speech. Now begins the Herculean task of amalgamating all the expectations and incorporating them in the speech and if success is to be achieved, well then, all the above mentioned expectations and many more need to be addressed.

Imagine using a similar strategy, for instance, in the organization for a presentation! When a presentation is made, the needs (intellectual) of the audience are kept in mind. There are not many variations in the audience expectations. Needs are simple but highly focused and revolve round information on tasks or methodologies of task/project completion. Ergo, the objective of the presentation zeros is on designing content with a focus on intellectual appeal.

In a presentation, the audience is always knit together by one common thread, be it department, organization, expectations, needs. This helps the presenter address a large group (20 or 25) in a focused manner. This is not the case with public speaking, where the group does not face the presenter as a single unit but as different components of an element each orbiting their own path.

Recently, a current belief has developed in the academia that to get the audience to listen to your content, first you have to arouse their emotions. They have to feel before they can listen and absorb. This methodology strongly advocates emotional appeal as the first step to intellectual affirmation/acceptance of the content. Our contention is not with the story-telling process but with the strategy of rousing the audience to a state from where there is no return. Sounds too strong? But that's how it is meant to be.

UNPLANNED PRESENTATIONS

Presentations can be planned as well as unplanned. The first category includes all those presentations of which you have prior knowledge and have had time to do research and conceptualize ideas.

In the unplanned category are the impromptu or extempore presentations. The two words are synonyms and can be used interchangeably. Under this category fall all those presentations in which you are summoned without advance notice and you need to talk on any issue on the spur of the moment.

If you are lucky, 10–15 minutes may be given to plan, structure and give a sequence to the ideas to be presented. But you can't always be lucky. You may be sitting in a large or a small group and suddenly out of the blue, without any warning, you are summoned to make additional contributions. For instance,

Ravi is the expert in computer networking. Ravi, we would like you to share your expertise with us.

Or

Vijay has done considerable research in the area of handling diversity in the organization. Vijay, can you please share some of your findings with our students?

You cannot refuse and there is almost no time to sit, reflect and structure ideas. Capitalize on thought speed. Utilize the time you take to reach from your chair to centre-stage to quickly strategize and chalk out the course of the impromptu speech.

Additionally, always have a couple of well-rehearsed humorous stories or anecdotes and quotes up your sleeve. They could be real, taken from some book or a joke at your own expense. Whichever story or anecdote you choose must be neutral, that is, without any religious, political or sexual connotations. The anecdote does not need to be terribly funny, but must contain light humour, sufficient to bring a smile to the audiences' faces. For instance,

The last time I was asked to speak, there was a power failure and we had to pack up and leave.

(Pause)

We have not had dinner. Hands up all those who still want me to continue.

Please remember the same jokes or statements cannot be used for different audiences. Imagine you have been summoned by the head of the R&D department in a presentation to the Board of Directors to talk about the state of research on a new cancer drug. You try the same communication with them as stated above. Believe me, no hands will go up and you will be generously treated with stony glares! Think of a different way to pick up the threads from where the R&D head left off.

If you have reached a certain position in life or the organization, you must be mentally tuned that you may be asked at any time to come up to the stage and speak. You have been working there for many years, so you will be familiar with the workings of your division or department. If you have been called to do this unplanned presentation, it is primarily because of your status and position in life or the organization.

The problem before you in these unplanned presentations is how to make them interesting. Read stories of achievers and leaders like, Krishna, Gandhi, Vivekanand, Ioccaca, Martin Luther, Napolean, Hitler. Anecdotes from their lives, and their perspectives can be used to begin almost any presentation. Let us assume that you have been called to make a brief presentation on a new project in the IT area and to motivate the team to perform to the hilt. You can, if you like, begin in this manner:

How many of you have read the Gita*? The opening dialogues between Krishna and Arjuna? Arjuna does not want to wage war against his cousins. It is Krishna who guides him and forces him to be goal oriented.*

Similarly, there is a goal before us and we must not get distracted. Our deadline for completion of this project is . . .

The same story can also be used in a 'call for action'. For instance, you have been called to talk to the disillusioned workers, who have not got their bonus.

How many of you have read the Gita? *The opening dialogues between Krishna and Arjuna? Arjuna does not want to wage war against his cousins. It is Krishna who guides Arjuna and tells him to DO his duty and not bother about the results. Rewards from the effort WILL follow. Today you are disillusioned and not willing to work. If you have belief in me and faith in what I say, continue with your duty and do not bother about the rewards or the fruits. Your work will not go unnoticed. . .*

You will notice that in both these instances, the story is the same. With a change in objective you have brought about a twist in the story. The point that I am trying to make is that if you are well versed with a few stories, you can always bring about the desired change so that it gels with the objective of the presentation.

Planning for unplanned presentations can begin at any stage, even now. Think of a situation. Give yourself 30 seconds to think and then begin speaking. The more you practice, the better honed will be your skills at attempting unplanned presentations. Some examples of situations can be as follows:

After having taken leave on grounds of ill-health, you are caught by your superior at a party. He is furious. Pacify him.

Your boss has prepared a report and you have detected certain errors. Point out the flaws in the report.

In a meeting a senior client asks for freewheeling of ideas. When you come up with bizarre ideas he makes fun of you in front of everyone. You are positively embarrassed and want to retort. How would you tackle a situation of this sort?

While making a presentation you see that the attention of the participants is wandering. What strategies do you adopt to solicit their attention?

You have an important issue to be discussed with your boss. He gives you time and when you start speaking you realize that he is preoccupied. Explain your point. Get the boss interested.

You have spent eight constructive hours on writing a report. Your boss chucks it aside saying it is useless. Discuss the issue.

The chairman of your organization sends for you seeking some information about the client. You are unaware of the minute details. You cannot reveal your ignorance as it would affect your promotion. Cover up the situation.

The more bizarre the situation, the better it is. Train yourself to think and talk in all sorts of situations (for more examples see Chapter VI). The logical ones then are easy to tackle.

PLANNED PRESENTATIONS

There are multiple types of planned presentations including informative, persuasive, direct reporting, and face-to-face or one-to-one presentations. They are explained below.

Informative and Persuasive Presentations

An informative presentation is one in which details and facts are provided and a persuasive attempt is made to influence the audience to a similar pattern of thinking. Informative presentations educate or inform the audience. Persuasive presentations allow you to sell an idea or make a sales pitch to the audience. Both presentations are different in terms of objective, design, and structure. The difference in objective guides the design and structure of the presentation. For example:

> *Your pharmaceutical company has developed a new drug. As part of the research team, you have to make a presentation to the inspection team on the formula and characteristics of the drug. This is an informative presentation. When you have to make a presentation to doctors of the district to persuade them to prescribe the medicine, it becomes a persuasive presentation.*

An informative presentation is fairly simple to plan and execute. Collate and compile the data, give it a structure and presto, it is ready to be delivered. In comparison, persuasive presentations are complex and need research, planning and structuring.

Persuasive presentations are a plea to the audience to change their pattern of thinking, and focus on the new manner of approach. Trying to figure out what will help the audience overcome its objections is the first step in the process of planning a persuasive presentation. It is not as easy as it sounds. The audience will have a fixed notion of what they want to know and what they know. When the audience listens to a presentation, the first thought in its mind is to decipher: what is the benefit to be derived from this presentation? In other words, what's in it for them (WIIFT)? You will have to patiently and emphatically spell it out and then reason with them—present the market situation, the competitor's share, the scarce opportunities—all will need to be stressed. In other words, apply any and every technique to cajole the audience to listen to the presentation.

Spelling out benefit statements is another strategy for making the audience sense the merit in the presentation. In a corporate presentation, issues that attract the attention of the audience revolve round actual, hidden, opportunity and estimated costs, risks, opinions of market leaders and competitors and the factor of time and deadlines. If you can deal with any or all of these, your presentation will be a success.

Finally, your authority or expertise in the area will make the audience focus on the content of the presentation.

Direct Reporting

Presentations can also be in the form of direct reporting to the superior, which is a one-to-one or face-to-face communication. Let us consider a few examples: Your immediate superior has recently joined the organization and would like you to prepare a report on the existing HR policies. Or, you have been working on the competency model for the company and the HR head wants you to present a direct report. Or, your HR head may summon you to his cabin requesting you to bring all papers pertaining to the employee appraisal system.

Let us consider another scenario. You have recently organized a mega-fair for your institute and need to make a presentation on the financials to the director or dean.

In all these situations, the presentation will be made to only one person seated in front of you. The strategies adopted in this case are different and intense, where you cannot take recluse to slides. It is more in the nature of a face-to-face talk with minimum frills. Accuracy and completeness of data, and clarity of thought are important. While in other presentations, it is the responsibility of the presenter to figure out the needs/expectations of the audience, in this case, the presenter is specifically told about the expectations. Hence, there can be no deviations from the stipulated path. It is advisable to check, recheck the points and the sequential arrangement for maximum impact.

Small Group and Large Group Presentations

All these different types of presentations can be made to large or small groups. Large groups can comprise 20 or 25 members and small groups can be as small as three or five members. While preparation for larger groups is tougher, because you need to research more on the audience, the presentation process is easier than for a small group.

There are many contradictory parameters to be considered while preparing for both large and small groups. More variety in the style and nature of presentation is required in a large group. You have to keep all the members awake, asking for more while listening. However, it is simple as your attention is diverted by and to a number of people.

The same cannot be said of a small group presentation which is high in intensity. There are fewer people to divert your attention to and the focus of the audience members is constantly on you. Questions and interaction are limited. Content has to be dense, of course in line with the expectations of the audience members. You have to be extremely alert and sharp to the responses of the audience. There are fewer interjections and lesser interaction. Even if you decide to make the presentation interactive, it is finally driven by your zeal and enthusiasm.

This is not to say that small group presentations are to be shunned. They are definitely a challenge which you can easily overcome by following all the techniques discussed in this book.

SUMMARY

1. Presentations are ideas, concepts or issues that are talked about or spoken to a group of people or an audience.
2. Understand the needs and expectations of the audience, listen to their ideas and weave them in self-generated concepts and talk/present.
3. Measure the success of the presentation by the identification of merit in the talk by the audience.
4. Public speaking and presentations both require oratory skills. The semblance between them ends at this point.
5. Unplanned presentations are the impromptu or extempore presentations.
6. Planned presentations are those in which you have prior knowledge and have had time to do research and conceptualize ideas.

7. Informative presentation is one in which facts are detailed.

8. Persuasive presentation is an attempt to influence the audience to a similar pattern of thinking.

Chapter II

Planning a Presentation

A good plan is like a road map: it shows the final destination and usually the best way to get there.

—H. Stanely Judd

If I had eight hours to chop down a tree, I'd spend six sharpening my axe.

—Abraham Lincoln

OBJECTIVES

- ❑ Identify factors essential for planning
- ❑ Determine the needs of the audience
- ❑ Develop material suited to audience requirement
- ❑ Structure and develop the content logically and sequentially

Key Words	
Audience	Objective
Audience analysis	Open-ended questions
Audience expectations	Purpose

Closed questions	Rhetorical questions
Cue cards	Sequential arrangement
Handouts	What
Logic tree	Where
Logical arrangement	Who
Material, Audience, Self	Why
(MAS)	When
	How

INTRODUCTION

'I have a presentation to make.'

'When?'

'Today.'

'Have you planned for the presentation?'

'Where is the need? I have been working in this department for the last five years and I know the functioning of the department inside out. I can speak. I know what I am supposed to say.'

Confidence, bordering on over confidence, is the death knell for presenters and presentations of all sorts. Preparation/planning for the big show is the first step on the ladder to success. Back it up with a positive approach, and the targets will become achievable.

The preliminaries involved in the process of making a presentation revolve around the not too interesting round of PLANNING. View this process or exercise as a game— a game of exercising control over MAS—the Material, the Audience and the Self. Adherence to the principles and practices of MAS will help in planning, structuring, and designing of content and visual aids; preparation of handouts; and analysis of audience.

The first commandment for planning a presentation— *Develop a positive attitude to presentations.*

Before the concept of MAS can actually be internalized, a question automatically springs to mind: 'History is replete with examples of powerful leaders who were also superb orators and presenters. Did they also exercise control over the MAS?' Names like Napolean and Hitler come to mind when we think of gifted orators, who had the ability to address a large crowd, without the slightest hesitation or nervousness. Unfortunately, leaders of a similar calibre are few. While it is easy to follow them, it is difficult to emulate their qualities. Acquiring or learning the same skills is tough and requires intensive training which will set the trainee apart from the rest of the crowd. The first step in the learning process is to exercise control.

Domain knowledge and subject expertise are an advantage but the game of presentation does not end at this point. Knowledge of the subject and the content are important but equally important is the control over the self and the audience. A scientific approach to planning is the best possible strategy. There is no research to corroborate the fact, but roughly speaking, adhering to scientific techniques of planning upgrades the quality of the presentation, enhances confidence and brings success 80 per cent of the time.

Let us draw an analogy to understand the need for planning. Why did the *Titanic* sink? Many reasons have been attributed for the tragedy. One of them was the inability to gauge the magnitude of the iceberg against which the *Titanic* collided, as only one-tenth of an iceberg is visible on the surface, a grim fact which was overlooked.

A presentation is like an iceberg. In other words, the delivery is only a tiny part. The major chunk of the presentation, visible only to a sensitive audience, is the time and effort spent in planning and preparing the presentation.

The second commandment for planning a presentation—*Preparing thoroughly for the success of the presentation is contingent on the enormous amount of preparation that precedes it.*

To create and deliver a successful presentation, you can and must take the support of the 'six helpers' commonly referred to as the five W's and the one H.

Six Helpers

The prime objective here is to identify the factors that help in effective planning, designing, and delivering of a presentation.

Simple though it sounds, a presentation involves lots of research, thought and structure. Beginning on the premise that the six helpers (i.e., the five W's and one H) promote and enhance the quality of the presentation, we need to build further on this proposition for better comprehension and satisfactory results.

The six helpers are interlinked and cannot be compartmentalized into separate categories. There are overlaps which make them interdependent and the presenter independent enough to prepare, deliver and win acclaim.

The six helpers/factors are listed in Table II.1:

Table II.1: Six Helpers

Helpers	What Does it Mean?
Who	Who is your audience?
What	What do you want to present (content)?
Why	Why do you want to present (purpose)?
Where	Where do you want to present (place)?
When	When do you want to present (time)?
How	How do you want to present (words used or avoided, slides used or avoided)?

Who

'Who' refers to the target audience for whom the presentation is prepared. Knowledge about the audience, including their needs, expectations, likes and dislikes, helps in structuring the presentation in an effective manner. Answers to the following questions will help in developing a presentation ideally suited to the needs of your audience.

Ask yourself the following questions:

Who is my audience?
What does the audience already know?
What does the audience need to know?
What is the experience of the audience?
What are their needs, expectations from this presentation?
How will the audience benefit from this presentation?

Let us begin by answering these questions. The audience is the top management of the firm. All members in the audience have a minimum of seven years of work experience in the same organization and they are familiar with the vision, mission, the basic policies and principles governing the firm. If you are a member of the marketing team and need to make a presentation to the top management, their needs and expectations would centre round the financial implications of the marketing strategies that you present. They will only be hooked on to the presentation when they sense that they are able to derive benefit from it.

With a change in the audience profile, the structure of the presentation also undergoes a change. If you are a member of the marketing team and a presentation has to be structured for the general manager and the marketing department team members, your focus will be on the implementation of the marketing strategies for the launch of a product.

> *Warning!* **A change in the profile of the audience necessitates a change in the structure of the presentation.**

Example

You are an assistant product manager in a pharmaceutical company, working in the corporate office with branches across 15 cities. The corporate office has asked you to prepare a presentation on one of the newly launched drugs in cardiovascular segments, its benefits and its effectiveness vis-à-vis other drugs already present in the market.

You have learned that the audience comprises senior managers from the sales division of the 15 branch offices. Their needs, on further analysis, reveal that their primary concern will revolve around convincing doctors that they should prescribe the drug, though it is more expensive than the one launched by the competitor six months ago. The reason for a higher price is better results and less side effects than the drugs already prevalent in the market.

Since they are sales managers, you must present the information relevant to them, by providing the right balance between technical information about the effectiveness of the drug, as well as the points which will help them convince the doctors to switch to this newly launched drug.

The third commandment for planning a presentation—
Assess the audience profile, their needs, expectations, likes and dislikes at the time of planning a presentation.

What

'What' or the content of the presentation should be the second concern addressed by the presenter. A specific content list should be chalked out by both the audience and the presenter. Ideally, the members of the audience must inform the presenter of their expectations from the presentation. In instances when this information is not available the presenter has a double task ahead:

- To gauge/find out the needs of the audience
- To structure the content keeping the needs of the audience in mind

Let us begin by taking a look at the second point first. Jot down on a piece of paper the answers to the following questions:

What do you want to tell your audience?

What is your objective?

A well-thought out one-liner is a response to all these queries. For instance, your objective can be to inform the audience of your impressive contribution in enhancing the growth in sales and indicate awareness of its financial implications. Another strategy for ascertaining accuracy in defining the 'what to tell' is reflection and an attempt to seek an answer to your own expectations from the presentation.

Example

You are working as a teacher in one of the reputed schools in the neighbourhood and your target audience is the local group of principals. You have introduced a new course which has caused ripples in the academic world. Your purpose of communicating with the

> *principals of schools is to give them details of the new*
> *module. Your purpose is to inform and convince them*
> *to introduce the course in their respective schools.*
>
> *The presentation, to be a value add, has to be a com-*
> *bination of information and persuasion—information*
> *on the course and persuasion that the course be intro-*
> *duced for the benefit and growth of the students.*

The fourth commandment for planning a presentation—*Work on the purpose, the objective of making*
a presentation.

In case you do not have sufficient information on the needs
of the audience, a study of their profile will help you in
understanding what can be their expectations from the
presentation.

In the above example, information that principals of
schools will attend the presentation, is sufficient for you
to gauge that their focus/interest will be double pronged:
a content presentation leading to implementation of
strategies.

> ***Just a Minute!* Have you worked on the ob-**
> **jective of the presentation?**

Why

While the 'what to tell' in a presentation can be outlined
in a single sentence, the purpose or 'Why' of the presentation requires much thought. The individual/collective
motive of the presenter is an answer to the following
questions:

- Why am I making this presentation?

- What is the purpose of making the presentation?
- Is the purpose to educate, inform, convince or train?

With a change in the purpose there is also a change in the structure of the presentation. For instance, in an educative presentation multiple perspectives are provided; in an informative one, statements, facts and figures are detailed; in a persuasive presentation, the attempt is to make a sales pitch or to sell the product by highlighting the merits and benefits; and finally in a presentation meant essentially for the purpose of training, the content is structured so as to solicit interaction and participation from the participants.

The members of the audience can and should inform the presenter of the necessity for making a presentation. Clarity in the initial phases of preparation/planning the purpose makes structuring simpler.

The fifth commandment for planning a presentation—
Seek an answer to the question 'why'. It will bring clarity in the content design and make the presentation credible.

Example

A presentation is to be made to the company staff on computerization being undertaken in all the regional offices.

Purpose: To demonstrate how computerization will enable them to work faster and more efficiently.

Where

The venue 'where' the presentation is to be made is equally important. Care must be exercised specifically with respect to the following two issues:

- The seating arrangement, and
- The lighting arrangement

Where you make a presentation is a major concern to be addressed in advance by the presenter. The room must be well-lit so that the audience can see you clearly. All wires and chords must be safely taped to the floor. You must arrive at the venue much in advance. Test your slides, go to the back of the room and see if the screen and the content on the screen is clearly visible. If there is too much light and you feel that the audience will have to crane its neck to catch a glimpse of the written content, the impact of the presentation will be lost.

The seating arrangement must also be organized so that there is enough elbow space for the participants. The best seating arrangement for easy viewing is a gently sloping U-shape. The U-shape allows both the presenter and the audience to observe one another and establish eye contact.

Example

> *If the audience is one customer, then the presentation can be informal, face-to-face in which you present the product to the customer. However, the case is different when the presentation is organized for a group of customers. You are making a sales pitch and your attempt is to reach out to all the customers. A U-shaped seating arrangement will be useful in establishing eye contact with all members of the audience. Additionally, you also get an opportunity to move in the centre aisle and narrow the distance between yourself and the audience.*

The sixth commandment for planning a presentation—
Arrive at the venue well in advance and make necessary and suitable changes.

When

The time, or 'when' are you making a presentation is an additional dimension to be considered at the planning stage. The three components that are essential to understand the 'when' factor are:

- The market condition
- The analysis of the situation
- The time when the presentation is to be delivered

Ask yourself the following questions:

- When will the presentation be made?
- Has there been a recent fluctuation in the market?
- Is the analysis accurate, current and to the point at the time of the presentation?

Warning! Do not make a presentation when the time is not ripe.

Often a presentation goes awry for the simple reason that it is delivered at the wrong time or the audience is not in the right mood. If the mood of the audience members can be gauged at the time of the presentation many an unhappy situation can be saved. For instance, a Friday evening, when all employees are in a weekend mood, is not a very appropriate time for making a sales pitch!

Example

Several cola drinks have been introduced in the market in the last six months. Your company would also like to introduce another cola drink.

This is ideally not the appropriate time to launch the product. In case your company still decides that it would like to go ahead with the idea, then the product marketing strategy has to be intense.

Differences between your drink and those already available in the market have to be spelled out clearly. Additionally, benefits from your drink also need to be highlighted for capturing the market.

The seventh commandment for planning a presentation—*Assess the time when the presentation is to be made.*

How

Recently there has been much controversy over the use of PowerPoint. The issue under discussion is the role donned by the presenter. What is the role of the presenter in the course of the presentation? A facilitator, a technician or a lecturer? If the presenter decides to facilitate the discussion then, merely putting thought-provoking statements across to the audience is required. In the role of a technician, the presenter merely operates the multimedia presentation and lets the audience decide for itself the true import of the message. As a lecturer, the presenter stands behind the podium and delivers the well-prepared speech. Which role then is most suitable in meeting the requirements of 'how' a presentation has to be made? Preferably a combination of all three!

Decide on the tools and the techniques to be used in the presentation and ask the following additional questions:

- ❑ Will the presentation be technical or non-technical?
- ❑ Will the presentation be formal or informal?

❑ What strategies will impress the audience?
❑ What should be presented and how?

There is an interesting anecdote about an organization which asked a consulting company to send their ace presenter to speak on presentation skills to a group of advertising executives. The consulting company was explicitly informed that the presentation was to be more in the nature of an informal chat. However this point was missed by the company and the consultant came immaculately dressed and prepared with a PowerPoint presentation. The presentation was a miserable failure. The purpose of the presentation was defeated. The '*how*' did not match with the requirements of the company.

Note: Select the mode and the medium of presentation subsequent to an analysis of the audience.

The 'how' to make a presentation can also be accurately assessed by gaining information on the audience profile. With a change in the profile there also comes about a change in the 'how' of the presentation.

> *In the right key one can say anything. In the wrong key nothing: The only delicate part is the establishment of the key.*
>
> —George Bernard Shaw

Example

As a production manager on the quality control practices in a manufacturing unit you can use technical terms if the presentation is to be made to the production supervisor. However, if a similar kind of a presentation is to be made to a media delegation, you must use general terms which are easily understood by the media representatives.

The eighth commandment for planning a presentation—
Work extensively on the suitable methodology for planning and structuring a presentation.

Work based on the profile of the audience can only happen if there has been a proper and thorough audience analysis.

Analysing Your Audience

The objective here is to identify the needs of the audience.

The target audience can be of two types: familiar and unfamiliar. In the first instance, you can easily find out about the needs of the audience. Where the audience is unfamiliar, it is difficult to structure a presentation which will have both content and appeal. For instance, you may not know what puts them off or what gets them ticking. Do they have a good sense of humour? Will a joke lighten up their mood in the middle of a serious discussion, or will it put them off? What are they really looking for in this presentation? Are they a conservative audience or would they like a more innovative proposal? At times, the answer to these questions can hold the key to persuading the audience.

Spend some extra time to find out necessary details of the audience. Get in touch with people in the organization where the presentation is to be made, and discuss their requirements so that you can prepare a tailor-made presentation. Remember, it is not just logic which works. Personal likes and dislikes can also sway a person's mind one way or the other. The talk and discussion need not be formal. Gather all your resources to conduct a systematic and scientific audience analysis.

To be able to understand the concept better, let us take a look at the following example:

Example

You are the manager in a product development division. You have recently realized that your team needs some more time to work on the music system which your company is set to launch soon. A little more time will help you come out with a music system that will consume less electricity than those already in the market. Your audience is the senior management of the marketing and finance division.

If you begin your presentation with the technical details which have resulted in this problem, you will lose the audience even before you have persuaded them to give your team more time. Instead, you must discuss how additional time will help you reduce the electricity consumption.

Some steps in the research on audience analysis are:

1. Talk to the concerned person directly and find out the profile and requirements of the members of the audience.
2. Find out the names of the people who would be part of the group and then through a company directory get their designation and job profile.
3. Discuss with the concerned people their needs for the presentation, if any.
4. Get as much information on the company as possible so that it helps you in making the content specific and market driven.

5. Figure out the benefits to the individuals and the organization that will accrue, post-presentation (see Table II.2).

Just a Minute! **Have you collected enough information about what the audience is looking for?**

Table II.2: Criteria for Audience Analysis

Criteria	Description
Level of interest	What is the level of interest of the audience?
Level of information/knowledge	What is the information the audience possesses? What is the information it needs? What does it know?
Types of questions	What are the types of questions it can ask?

Level of Interest

Try to decipher the anticipated response pattern of the audience. Will the topic of presentation interest the audience members? For instance, if it is a sales pitch, are the clients interested in the low cost? Or are they more worried about the quality of the product. There is no point in talking about a budget to a client who is ready to pay more for quality or exclusivity. The topic of presentation has to be structured in such a manner that it elicits the best possible response from the audience in terms of interest.

To be able to develop interest in the presentation, try to come up with a specific rather than a general topic. A specific topic which addresses issues directly rather than leaves room for doubt is the best possible strategy to attract the attention of the audience and invite maximum participation.

Example

> 'Merits and Demerits of using XYZ ingredient in a skin care product', will be an appropriate topic for an audience comprising the research department of the company. Alternately, a presentation topic such as 'Launch of a skin care product', can have audience members across functions like marketing, sales, and finance.

Just a Minute: Is the material sufficiently interesting to hold audience attention for the entire duration of the presentation?

Level of Information/Knowledge

Determine the kind of information that will interest the audience. Clarity in your mind concerning *audience expectations* will aid in presentation development. The audience expectations will naturally be a result of the knowledge they possess or the information they have on the subject. Hence, it is a good idea to collect information about the profile of the participants, their experience in the company, their age, etc. This will help, to a great extent, in streamlining the content at the planning stage.

Based on the knowledge level, experience and job profile of the audience, you can, for instance, figure out which format will appeal to the audience. It may consist of:

Technical jargon
Statistical facts
Historical data
Market analysis
Demonstrations
Samples

Employees in the production department, for example, will be interested in technical jargon; research and development in historical data, demonstrations, samples; marketing people in statistical facts and market analysis, etc. You will notice that the level of interest is directly related to the job profile of the participants. Hence, a good strategy to figure out the level of information/knowledge that members of the audience possess is to find out more about their experience in the company and their job profile.

Warning! Keep the audience perspective in mind when using jargon and technical information

Also, be careful about the kind of assumptions you make with regard to the level of audience knowledge. If you get too technical while making a presentation to a group of non-technical people, they may just get bored.

> *It's not the plan that's important, it's the planning.*
> —Dr. Gramme Edwards

Or worse still, they may think that you are trying to be condescending by discussing issues they are unfamiliar with. This would prejudice their minds and the end result would be—no gains!

At the same time, a presentation which is too simple and non-technical can be seen as something which does not add value. An audience member might just feel, 'Hey, I know all this. Why should I listen to this person when he/she is just talking plain common sense?'

There is a very thin line between getting too technical and being simplistic in your approach. Take cues from the audience from their body language and gestures regarding their interest level.

Nature of Questions

Anticipate the **questions** that can be asked in the course of the presentation. A good presenter always leaves room for the participants to ask questions. Questions can be open-ended, close-ended or rhetorical.

Open-ended questions are those that make the discussion interactive and participative. For example, 'What are your views on leadership?'

Close-ended questions are those that expect only a 'yes' or a 'no' as an answer. 'Don't you think in moments of crisis one should act rather than think or debate.' If a close-ended question has been asked by an audience member, no time or opportunity will be given to the presenter to verbally answer the question. The irate or participative member of the audience will proceed with a presentation of points.

The third type of question is the rhetorical one, which is an extension of the close-ended questions. In this case, no answer is sought from the presenter. The purpose of these questions is to get the recipient of the message into the thinking mode. For instance, 'Do you think leadership exists any-

> *The very best financial presentation is one that's well thought out and anticipates any questions... answering them in advance.*
> —Arthur Helps

where in the world? In India? In your locality?' The person raising the query does not wait for a response but proceeds with the discussion.

All three types of questions must be anticipated and the presenter mentally prepared with responses to them. Fumbling or fidgeting for the right answer spoils the impact of the presentation. If you are planning for a presentation, familiarity with the profile of the participants, their requirements and the benefits they will gain from this presentation will aid you in anticipating the questions that might be posed.

> **Warning!** Do your homework. Have all the information you need to respond to possible questions.

Example

If you present 'Cost Saving Music Systems' to your customers, then some of the questions that can be raised are:

o *'How much will we save?'*
o *'What is the cost of existing music systems in the market?'*
o *'To what extent will we benefit if we purchase this music system?'*
o *'What are the benefits not present in other music systems?'*

Even a very well-structured and well-delivered presentation could leave a bad impact if the final question-answer session does not go well. Since this is the final impression your audience is going to carry about you, make sure your response is well received.

Collating Material

The objective here is to collate relevant material from various sources.

Working in a department or an organization does not necessarily make you the domain expert. There may be many people working in the department of an organization who would necessarily or naturally possess more knowledge or information than you do. How do you tackle, or handle this situation? Begin gradually by a thorough analysis of the audience. Mentally prepare yourself for the knowledge they possess and then begin collating material from various sources before you actually give it a structure.

Let us assume that the manager, corporate communications, has been asked to make a presentation to the president and vice president of the company on the corporate communications policies. The manager will need to talk to the PR manager, the advertising manager on the strategies and the policies, and the financial head on the budget allocated for corporate communications. It is only after all relevant material from these different sources is collated that a shape can be given to the presentation. Sometimes, the presenter may also need to do research for statistical details, and analysis before presenting the final recommendations.

Note: **Collate and structure presentation material based on audience analysis.**

The method of collation of material is a result of the analysis of audience needs. For instance, if the audience wants a detailed presentation on the financials of the company, then a study of the company and industry reports is the best possible source for collation of material.

There are various sources for collating material, such as:

1. The Internet
2. The company library
3. In-house magazines
4. Reports

With the advent of technology, the Internet is the best possible source for information. On certain occasions you may also be expected to make technical presentations to clients on the use of components in certain products. Gathering information on the components then becomes a major task for you. Various libraries, technical books, and the Internet are good sources for collecting material. If a presentation is to be made for a client or a customer and sufficient information is not forthcoming, surf on the Net and you will be able to download more than sufficient information. However, caution must be exercised in the use of the Internet as companies do not always present a complete picture. You must collect the data and conduct your own analysis. This will make your information objective and relevant to the audience.

If you are part of the group in the organization in which the presentation is to be made, the in-house magazines and reports form the best possible source for data collection.

> *Before everything else, getting ready is the secret of success.*
> —Henry Ford

Analysis of information for the last five years gives you a complete picture and helps establish your credibility as a well-prepared presenter. In the process of borrowing from existing reports, exercise restrain and impose self constraint on the amount and nature of text that is borrowed which can extend to objective statement of facts. While the temptation is great to use the analysis and the recommendations, let that be a process following your own analysis.

Additionally, the company library provides a good source for collecting material. It contains substantial details of products, components, and market surveys, that will aid you, as a presenter, in formulating the text for the presentation.

Structuring Material

It is important to organize presentation material logically and sequentially.

The material for the presentation has been collated and you are now drowning in a plethora of facts and figures, some necessary and some unnecessary. Where to begin is the big question. How to give the material a logical shape? What information to include and what to exclude? What will appeal to the audience?

> The ninth commandment of planning a presentation—
> *Cool and collected thinking and structuring brings
> into focus the objective or purpose of the presenta-
> tion.*

Structuring of material is a two step process:

❏ Writing the points on cue cards and
❏ Preparing a logic tree

Begin the process of structuring the material by cutting out rectangular cue cards approximately the size of the palm with thick chart paper. From the collated material write only one point each on the cue card. Once all the points have been jotted down spread the cue cards on a table in front of you. By reading the cards on the table in front of you, try and work out the sequence which you think at this stage will appeal to the audience. This sequence is contingent on the needs and expectations of the audience.

What information will capture the attention of the audience?

What sequence of points must be followed so that the audience is able to sense a value add?

Answers to these questions will help you in numbering and arranging the cue cards in a sequence. It is important to number the cue cards so that accidentally two cards do not slip to the back of the pile while making the presentation. As you proceed, you can look at the points written on the cue cards and elaborate on them. After one point has been explained, slip the cue card you were using to the end of the stack and begin the next point (see Table II.3).

Table II.3: Structuring Material

o Cut out cue cards made of thick chart paper
o Write one point only on each cue card
o Spread all the cards on the table
o Arrange them in a logical order
o Number the cards
o Arrange them in a pack

With modern techniques of making presentations, all presenters carry a laptop or are provided with a computer and make presentations using a multimedia projector. While cue cards are not carried to the venue, beginning a preparation with cue cards facilitates structuring as points are arranged and rearranged, without much discomfort to the presenter, by merely shuffling the cards in a desired order.

After you are through with the sequential arrangement of the cue cards, prepare a logic tree to verify the logical flow in the presentation.

Example

You are working for a hospital equipment division in an organization. A new X-ray machine has been manufactured and you have been asked by the organization to make a sales pitch to the doctors of a local hospital.

The points that you have been able to assemble are:

- *Models of X-ray machines currently being used*
- *Approximate number of x-rays being done by the hospital in a year*
- *Distribution of usage across departments*
- *Degree of usage by various departments*
- *Costs involved*
- *Unique features of the machine*

Note: **Identify the purpose of the presentation and prepare a logic tree.**

These six points must be arranged in a sequential or logical order and in a fashion which appeals to the doctors. The points can be rearranged in the following ways (see Figure II.1):

- ❑ Logical
- ❑ Sequential

If you are unable to structure the points in a diagrammatic form, arrange them sequentially, as shown in Figure II.2.

In this example, you have to persuade the doctors to purchase the new X-ray machine. You begin the presentation by highlighting the benefits of the X-ray machine and then discuss the cost, which allows the doctors to see its value. Additionally, by discussing the frequency of use of the X-ray machines, you cover maintenance issues. This

Figure II.1: Logical Structuring of Points

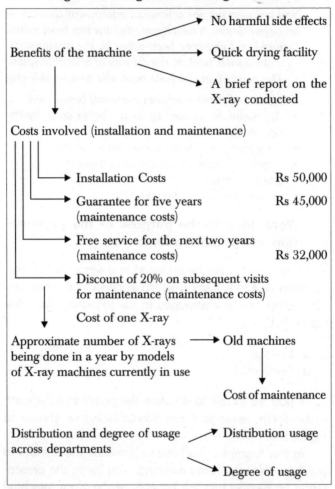

method allows you to reiterate facts and move into the domain of the audience for receptivity of message.

When you began structuring your presentation, you had an additional point called 'Models of X-ray machines

Figure II.2: Sequential Arrangement of Points

1. Benefits of the machine:
   - No harmful side-effects
   - Quick-drying facility
   - A brief report on the X-ray conducted

2. Costs involved (installation and maintenance)
   Rs 50,000 (installation costs)
   Guarantee for five years (maintenance costs)
   Rs 45,000
   Free service for the next two years (maintenance costs)
   Rs 32,000
   Discount of 20 per cent on subsequent visits for maintenance (maintenance costs)

3. Approximate number of X-rays being done in a year by models of X-ray machines currently in use
   Cost of one X-ray
   Old machines
   Cost of maintenance

4. Distribution and degree of usage across departments
   Distribution of usage
   Degree of usage

currently being used'. When the points were arranged in a logical sequence, a discussion on the models of X-ray machines currently being used was found to be redundant. However, to make the presentation comprehensive and complete, add point number 3, as indicated in the logic tree.

There are many presentations which last for barely 15 minutes and the audience is not able to recollect the main ideas in the presentation. At the same time there are other presentations which last for hours and the audience is able to recollect all that was said in the presentation. The success of the second type of presentations is a result of careful planning. Your presentation too can be a success, if a simple question is asked at the time of planning: 'Will the audience remember the presentation a week later?'

❑ If your honest answer is yes, then you are sure to be a success.

❑ However, if your honest answer is no, do not become reticent. Follow it up with additional questions:
  • 'Have I cluttered my presentation with too much text?'
  • 'Are there too many facts and figures?'
  • 'Am I giving the audience too much information?'
  • 'Did I structure my thoughts and ideas logically and sequentially?'

Answers to all these questions then, become the nodal points round which re-planning and redesigning takes place. In this second round follow up the planning with some additional questions:

❑ Does the presentation contain relevant information, i.e., is it relevant to the audience?

❑ Is the information, correct, and accurate?

❑ Does the information generate interest for the audience?

The tenth commandment of planning a presentation— *Provide only that much information as can be remembered by the audience.*

Planning is a process of asking questions and reflecting on issues to be discussed/presented. The more the number of questions asked, the higher is the probability of the presentation being error free. Many questions are asked at the stage of planning to make the presentation successful. It is better to resort to the question-answer technique at the planning and thinking stage than to fumble for the right words at the time of making a presentation. Research, analysis and structuring of data are the keys to being successful while facing a large or a small audience.

Have a plan. Follow the plan, and you'll be surprised how successful you can be. Most people don't have a plan. That's why it's is easy to beat most folks.
—Paul 'Bear' Bryant
football coach, University of Alabama's Crimson Tide.

Additionally as reflections are indicative of the thinking process, the more the reflections, greater is the probability of the presentation being a success.

Just a Minute! **Have you cluttered the slides with too much information?**

Preparing Handouts

Additional information can be provided to the audience in the form of handouts. For instance, if a presentation is to be made by the finance and accounts manager to the team members, projecting all figures on the screen does not serve any purpose. None will be able to retain the information. The details can be given to the audience members in the form of handouts. Give a one-page handout at the stage when excessive figures which cannot be projected on the screen are being discussed. The presenter can continuously keep drawing the attention of the audience to the points on the hand-out.

You have to be very careful with the use of handouts. If they are given before the presentation, the audience automatically begins to leaf through it and loses touch with you. Giving it at the end is a better strategy. The members can take the handouts with them and read it at leisure (which may or may not happen!).

| **Caselet** |

Hewlitt Software Manufacturers (HSM), Gurgaon
HSM, a Gurgaon based company, is in the business of software manufacturing and development. It has been in business for the last 20 years and has witnessed incremental profits in the past years.

You are the general manager, Human Resources. Apprise the Board of Directors of the fact that the high attrition in the company is a result of a lower salary paid by the company than the market median.

In the last year there has been a substantial drop in its profits as 20 per cent of its employees have been leaving the organisation in every quarter. The time, effort and costs involved in recruitment and training have been substantial and the payoff negligible. The primary cause for this is that younger employees are using the company as a training ground and stop-gap arrangement before they move on to greener pastures. The HR head has been asked by the Board of Directors to research the causes for the high attrition rate and to present the findings and make recommendations.

Let us analyse this case and work on the five Ws and the one H.

Who is my audience?

The audience comprises the Board of Directors of HSM.

What does the audience already know?

The audience knows the company history and its growth rate. It is also aware of the fact that the attrition rate in HSM is quite high and has led to a drop in its profits. They realize that the company needs to take pro-active steps to bring down the attrition rate.

What does the audience need to know?

The Board of Directors needs to know the reasons behind the high attrition rate. Is it comparable to the industry figures? If not, then why? What is the impact of high attrition rate on the company's bottom line? What are the costs involved in recruiting and training new employees? How much time does it involve? If the trend continues, how will it affect HSM?

Clearly, the younger employees are using the company as a training ground and stop-gap arrangement before they move on to better jobs. This is mainly because of the low pay package offered by HSM This key reason should be identified and communicated to the Board of Directors.

They also need to know the kind of job profile, pay package etc. that the HSM employees move on to. This should be linked with the company policies to see if HSM needs to make any changes in its functioning.

What is the experience of the audience?

The audience belongs to the top management of the company. This means that they would be considerably aware of what is happening in the company and where it is going. They also have the authority to take a call on whether the recommendations are useful and if they should implement them.

What are their needs, expectations from this presentation?

The audience would expect a formal, well-researched and well-prepared presentation from the GM. It would want an in-depth analysis of why the attrition rate is high in HSM. It would also expect a concrete recommendation and a detailed action plan by the HR department to bring down the attrition rate.

How will the audience benefit from this presentation?

The audience will be apprised of the reasons behind the high attrition rate and thus be able to make the necessary changes to address the issue.

Checklist for Planning a Presentation

Do's	*Don'ts*
Identify the six helpers—five Ws and one H	Don't try to compartmentalize the six helpers
Understand the interest level of the audience	Don't make too many assumptions about the audience
Use simple language	Don't use jargon if the audience doesn't understand it
Make the presentation focused, easy to understand	Don't get too simplistic in your presentation
Use secondary sources to collate information	Don't depend on secondary sources for in-depth analysis
Prepare cue cards	Don't forget a cue card and miss a point
Prepare a logic tree	Don't be rigid in following a sequence
Be prepared for any kind of question from audience	Don't bluff your way through the question
Understand the audience question clearly	Don't fumble or fidget while responding to questions
Provide handouts for additional information	Don't circulate handouts before the presentation

SUMMARY

1. Use the six helpers to plan the presentation.
2. Understand the purpose of the presentation.
3. Think about what it is that you would like to say.
4. Work out the time when you would be making a presentation.
5. Analyse the medium you would need to deliver the presentation.
6. Check the venue you will be using for the presentation.
7. Assess the needs of the audience before planning the presentation.
8. Anticipate the questions which can be close-ended, rhetorical or open-ended.
9. Prepare responses to the questions.
10. Collect material from a variety of sources.
11. Arrange points logically or sequentially.
12. Be well-prepared with handouts which you may need to use in the course of the presentation.

Chapter III

Structuring a Presentation

To know what to leave out and what to put in; just where and how, ah, THAT is to have been educated in the knowledge of simplicity.

—Frank Lloyd Wright.

Structure is more important than content in the transmission of information.

—Abbie Hoffman

OBJECTIVES

- ❑ Identify needs of the audience
- ❑ Assess the nature of the presentation
- ❑ Develop a structure for the presentation
- ❑ Identify and use strategies
- ❑ Adopt a variety of techniques

Key Words	
Agenda	Declaration
Anecdote narration	Facts and figures

Capability of the audience	Informative presentations
Channels	Jokes/humour
Clarity	Middle
Closing	Opening
Credibility	Persuasive presentations
Consistency	Questions
Content	Quotations
Content development	Scenario description
Context	Strategies

INTRODUCTION

The prelude is finally over! Now begins the task of giving shape/structure to the planned processes. Many are of the view that structuring is a simple process because the thinking has already been done. Unfortunately, it is a misnomer as the thinking begins in the second phase, once all the material has been collated.

In the first stage, that is the planning stage, the work is collation of material and information. Structuring, which requires much understanding and thinking, is a subsequent step and begins with an understanding and analysis of the audience needs and expectations. Remember the key to success in any presentation is the ability to hold the attention of the audience. Bring about an alignment between the expectations of the audience and the structure of the presentation and the day is won even before the commencement of the battle. What is the process then to be followed?

Adherence to the 7Cs is the initial step in gaining credence in your presentation.

1. Credibility

2. Context
3. Content
4. Clarity
5. Channels
6. Consistency
7. Capability of the audience

The first commandment of structuring a presentation—
Analyse the needs and expectations of the audience.

Credibility

How credible are you, as a presenter? What is the level of trust you share with the audience? Be aware of your perceived knowledge level, especially if you are making a technical presentation. You need to know if the audience will accept your analysis because of your expertise, or whether they will question your assumptions.

Two factors that help you to gain credibility with the audience are position and authority. However, it does not mean that if you are not in an enviable position you will not be able to gain credibility. You too can develop content-rich and context-loaded presentations simply by adhering to the rules of the other six Cs.

For example, a student can gain credibility by delivering an informative presentation which contains accurate representation of required facts and figures.

Context

Why are you making this presentation? What is the context? Is it an in-house or an external presentation? Try to understand the audience, its expectations and the context in which the presentation is to be made. You need to be aware of the implications of your presentation as well as the recommendations you may make. The receptivity of the audience to your message will be moulded by their needs. For example, if you were asked to make a presentation on the achievements of the company to the marketing team at the time when they are planning strategies for the launch of a product, the time and the context will be inappropriate. Chances are dim that they will even listen to what you are saying or presenting.

Content

Are you thorough with the content that needs to be presented? Have you done enough research on the subject, on the topic? You may be an ace presenter but to be successful in a presentation it takes more than oratory skills to succeed. Let us for a minute assume that when it comes to working on the cost benefit analysis you are not very good. You have read a couple of articles on the subject and have volunteered to teach some students the process by which cost benefit analysis can be done. While presenting this topic in the class, you realize that you are not able to proceed. The content that you may wish to present may be theoretical and the needs of the students may be to get more practical orientation. The uncertainties in your mind,

> *Reduce your plan to writing. The moment you complete this, you will have definitely given concrete form to the intangible desire.*
>
> —Napoleon Hill

the loose ends will make the content presentation superficial and mar the impact of the presentation.

On the other hand, if the presentation is content heavy which is difficult for the audience to grasp, problems will surface. In both situations receptivity of the audience will be minimal.

Clarity

Are you clear about what is it that you wish to present or have been asked to present? Is there clarity in your thinking process? Is there a clear structure that you follow in your presentation? It is not enough to merely provide the content, it has to be structured and presented in a logical, clear sequence. At no point in the presentation must the audience begin to feel or sense that they have lost touch with the content. This situation can arise only when you begin jumping from one point to the other, or bringing in unrelated facts that create confusion in the minds of the audience. Be clear about what you want to convey and focus continuously on it throughout the presentation.

Suppose you have been asked to make a presentation to the management students on 'Presentation Skills'. You begin by talking about the need to be convincing and move on to similarities between conviction abilities in negotiations and presentations. You try and pick up the threads of 'Presentation Skills' and demonstrate the need for assertive behaviour while facing the audience. The time spent facing the audience is equally divided between developing the three skills: presentation, negotiation and assertiveness. The audience is left in a dilemma. Was the presentation on developing 'Presentation Skills' or 'Negotiation Skills' or 'Assertiveness'?

> The second commandment of structuring a presentation—*Be crystal clear in your thinking process and content development.*

Channel

Which channel would you like to use for the transmission of your message to the audience? It could be audio, visual or multimedia. There can be only one criterion for the selection of a channel—will the channel be appropriate for an a-type of audience?

If you decide to use only the audio channel, the audience will not be able to view you, hence the attention that you could have commanded by your physical presence will be missing. More work will then have to be put in voice modulations and content development. Similarly, if it is just the visual medium, structuring of the visual content will have to be worked in a manner so as to solicit maximum attention and retention. If you are lucky and have the opportunity of using multimedia, use your creative capabilities, but only to the extent that they match the requirements of the audience.

Consistency

Do you consistently follow a story line? Are you focused in your approach? It is simple for the audience to follow the content of the message if you are consistent in your approach. Consistency follows directly from clarity. If you are clear in your mind on what is it that you wish to project, consistency will naturally follow. You will be able to identify links and connections. Any kind of internal in-consistencies or disparity in views will severely affect your reliability. Avoid any confusion regarding the analysis and the final recommendation. For example, while discussing institutional policies, the director of an institute empha-sizes that faculty producing research papers published in peer reviewed journals will be given an opportunity to at-tend international conference every quarterly and within a few seconds of this announcement stresses the need for outlining a stringent budget for the financial year. As a member of the faculty team you will be left wondering which of the two statements to believe.

To be credible, a similar pattern of thought must be adopted—either stringent measures have to be incorpo-rated in the budget or leeway has to be given to the faculty on the basis of work produced.

The third commandment for structuring a presentation— *Prepare a story line and follow it consistently in the presentation.*

Capability of the Audience

Do not under- or overestimate the capability of the audi-ence you are addressing. Incorrect assessment of the audi-ence and underestimation of their knowledge level and their position would stagnate the efforts you put in the preparation and make the presentation boring, without any zing! On the other hand, if you overestimate and be-gin to use technical jargon with a non-technical audience, you have lost the day and the presentation. Your audience is unable to 'connect' with you or your talk. Worse still, they can even take offence thinking that you are trying to be condescending.

In this chapter, you will learn about the following:

1. Parts of a Presentation
   o The beginning/opening
   o The middle
   o The end/closing
2. Presentation boosters

Parts of a Presentation

The topic objective is to structure a presentation effectively.

A presentation is a linear progression of an idea, a concept structured in a logical manner. There is a story line and like any story the main episodes have to be 'told' or narrated to the audience. There are three parts to a presentation:

- Beginning/opening
- Middle
- End/closing

As is well known, in the opening or the beginning the presenter 'tells' the audience what is to come or what to expect; in the middle 'tells' them what was promised in the opening; and in the closing reiterates or 'tells' them the ideas that have been presented.

The most crucial part of the presentation is the beginning. You introduce the topic, set the pace, capture the attention of the audience, and establish credibility. The closing is the second most critical part. Whatever is said at the end of the presentation is what the audience takes back with them. The importance attached to the opening and closing of the presentation must not negate the value of the middle section of the presentation. In the middle section, the central idea is presented. The structure, the logic, and the authenticity of the presentation are established in this section.

Just a Minute! **Have you thought through the structure of the presentation carefully?**

In a 30-minute presentation, the average break-up of time for the various sections is as follows:

- 2 to 2.5 minutes—beginning/opening
- 21 to 22 minutes—middle section
- 1 to 2 minutes—end/closing
- 5 minutes—question-answer session or interaction/ discussion with the audience

Of course, it goes without saying that this is only a suggested guideline. There may be minor variations in time but overall the time allocated to the opening and the closing is the same.

The Beginning/Opening

The objectives here are to:

- introduce the presentation topic to the audience through various techniques; and
- capture the attention of the audience

The opening is designed keeping the profile of the participants in mind. Structuring the opening is easier if you begin with the positive thought that the presence of the audience is an indicator that the audience is really interested in listening to the presentation. Now begins your task of getting them to stay hooked to the content. Sounds simplistic, but gets tougher when you assign yourself the task of designing strategies. Application of attention-gaining strategies should be done right in the beginning of the presentation. Complacency arising out of working in the organization for many years can mar the quality and content of the presentation. If you want the process to be easy, begin structuring the presentation, imagining that the members of the audience have been sitting, listening to presentations from 9.00 am and your turn comes at 7.00 pm. The audience is tired and mentally exhausted and tuned to non-organizational issues like traffic jams, and outings with the family.

How will you begin in this scenario? What will you say? How will you deliver your content to be able to capture their attention? Think carefully through the opening/beginning, weave in creativity, relate it to the main objectives of the presentation and tailor it to suit their requirements.

The fourth commandment of structuring a presentation—*Work and rework on the opening of the presentation.*

Various strategies can be used for the beginning/opening of a presentation that can capture the attention of the audience, if used in appropriate measure. These strategies are listed below:

- Anecdote narration
- Scenario description
- Jokes/Humor
- Facts and figures

- Quotations
- Questions
- Declaration
- Agenda

While all these strategies are innovative and much better than the usual 'Good morning Ladies and Gentlemen. The topic for my presentation today is ...' the most powerful of these are anecdote narration and scenario description.

***Just a Minute!* Have you planned your opening?**

Anecdote Narration

Narrating an anecdote or a story is the most powerful device that can be used either in the opening or middle of the presentation. The power of the story to hold the attention is unparalleled. Reminds one of folk lores structured on this basic principle.

Try this technique! The member of the audience may be a child of two or a busy executive of 30 years. The minute you begin telling a story, their attention and the floor is all yours. You can make the story interesting enough to keep them hooked for hours, or boring enough to forego their attention in a few minutes. In fact, this is such a powerful device that many CEOs use this method to present facts and situations in the form of a story which has universal or organizational appeal.

The use of an anecdote at the beginning of the presentation must be made with caution. It is immaterial whether the anecdote is one with which the audience is familiar or unfamiliar. What is relevant is that the presenter must be able to relate it to the main objective of the presentation.

Example

You have been working in the R&D department of a pharmaceutical company for the last five years. You have been asked by your manager to convince the team members of the need to put in extra work for a new anti-aids drug. You begin by telling them a story: 'Not so many years ago, I was working in Africa. I had been there for five years and during my initial stay I made friends with an automobile engineer. He too was from India and we became the best of friends. As time passed I realized he was suffering from AIDS. We tried all possible medication but nothing could save him. I remember the day when he passed away, in tremendous pain in my arms ...

After my friend's painful death I vowed that I would work in a pharmaceutical company and develop new drugs to fight the worst of diseases. Today, I present my new formulae and new ideas ... but I need your support. Alone, I cannot fight death ... together we can .....

Scenario Description

A scenario description is an extension of an anecdote narration. In this strategy, the presenter extends the scope of the story by bringing to life the environment in which the episode or story happened. In scenario description, there is more build up of visual imagery to give the listener a feel of the atmosphere in which the narrated incident occurred. While an anecdote narration focuses more on the content of the narrative, a scenario description specifically concentrates on the description of the event and the protagonists. Use of adjectives and adverbs like 'tense', 'herculean', 'hot', 'mostly', 'scarcely' are used to make the description appealing to the audience members. The principle on which scenario description operates is that it stimulates the senses of the members of the audience and secures their attention. Additionally, we can also say that a scenario description is like a movie clip, in which the viewer watches the action and movements of the protagonist or the processes in which the story is embedded. Similarly, in a scenario, the audience gets a glimpse of the real world through an appropriate choice of words.

Example

For the same example stated above, you might start with: 'My friend, an automobile engineer in Africa was suffering from AIDS. Have you ever seen a victim of AIDS? Thin, weak, eyes bulging out, stomach caved in, lack of energy . . . have seen my friend suffer as he breathed his last in my arms.'

Jokes/Humour

Using jokes or humor is a good strategy for beginning a presentation. However, it can backfire. The joke may not appeal to the audience, causing the connection between the presenter and the audience to break. For instance, if a presentation is being made in a cross-cultural environment, it is good to be conventional. Businesses are going global and with counterparts in all parts of the world, presentations are made to diverse groups comprising people from, say, Germany, England, France, America etc. It is very difficult to speak the same language as them, let alone understand their sense of humour or bring about a harmonious blend between these people belonging to different nationalities. Sheer politeness may make them tolerant of your deviations from the main content but the situation would be pathetic if the amusement on their faces was a byproduct of the sympathy they experienced for the presenter.

The experience and seniority of the members of the audience must also be considered when using jokes or humour. For instance, if it is a presentation for the Board of Directors and you decide to begin the presentation with a joke, two minutes of their precious time has been wasted. Their need from the presentation probably was an in-depth understanding of the financials involved in a current project. In all probability, they have another presentation or meeting lined up. The joke falls flat and you begin amiss stony glares from members of the audience. The purpose of designing a creative opening to a presentation is defeated.

When in doubt of the receptivity of the audience to a joke, adhere to the safe path by using a traditional opening, in which the topic is introduced, benefits of the ideas specified and the presentation rounded off. However, if you are aware of the audience, their likes and dislikes and feel you can present a joke to get the audience involved, go ahead.

Warning! **Do not incorporate irrelevant matter and vulgar jokes.**

Facts and Figures

People across the globe are caught up with facts, figures and number crunching. As per Edward De Bono's use of six hats, the most appealing is the white hat, which is neutral and carries stark facts and figures. Let us take a look at the significance of numbers/facts/figures which you may use in the course of the presentation.

Compare the two statements:

'The company suffered major losses a couple of years back.'

'The company suffered losses to the tune of five crores in the year 2003.'

Which of the two statements do you think has more appeal? Definitely the second statement. The first statement is vague, as it gives us no clear picture of the amount of losses and the year. In the second statement you have used numbers to attract attention and have also been specific instead of vague. The second statement is precise and leaves no room for doubt. Finally, the second statement prepares the audience for what is to follow. In this particular example you have discussed what happened in the year 2003, and will probably proceed with an explication of what happened to the losses: whether they were recovered or whether they multiplied.

The relevance of this opening must be clearly understood before it is applied to any presentation. On many occasions the audience is familiar with the numbers or statistics provided. This opening then loses its significance. Facts and figures must be startling or new and not old. Use facts and figures to capture the attention of the audience. In instances when the audience is familiar with the *statistics* or figures used in the presentation, and you still sense the need for projection of those figures, make the analysis new or novel. The novelty of the analysis must be captivating and lead to the development of the case in the presentation. Views can be supported with the help of graphs or charts.

Example

The facts and figures can be shown somewhat as follows:

1980 : XYZ Company established
1985 : XYZ introduced micro motors
1987 : Sales went up

Quotations

When are quotations used? You can incorporate quotes in the opening section when you sense that the logical development of a point can be better appreciated by the audience if it is supported by impressive statements made by leaders or veterans. As a concept, the idea is unparalleled. The problems begin when the concept is applied on stage. If the quote is very long, it will be difficult for you to remember the piece and you will have to turn around to read from the screen or read from a chit of paper. In the process of delivering the quote, direct eye contact with the audience is lost. If this happens at the opening of a presentation, it is very difficult getting the attention of the audience back to the presentation.

Let us consider the following three examples:

Example

1. *Of the best rulers*
   The people (only) know that they exist
   The next best they love and praise
   The next they fear
   And the next they revile
   But (of the best) when their task
   Is accomplished, their work done
   The people all remark, 'We have done it ourselves'.

Lao Tse

2. *Always bear in mind that your own resolution to succeed is more important than any one thing.*

Abraham Lincoln

3. *If A is success in life, then A equals x plus y plus z. Work is x, y is play and z is keeping your mouth shut.*

Albert Einstein

The first quote while interesting to read, is too long. The second is simple, and the third is mathematical. You have to make a choice between the three quotes. Which one to choose and which two to reject? The length of the first quote becomes the determining factor for elimination. You are now left with a choice to be made between the second and the third quote. Which quotation would you choose for your presentation? The choice depends on the topic and the level of the audience. The quotation can be borrowed from any discipline; what is important is that it must help develop the points.

What is the merit of using quotations in the opening section of the presentation? Quotations act as a point of reference for establishing the case. A quote can be a statement or several statements made by a renowned personality that help develop a case. Preferably, only single sentence quotes should be used which can be memorized and stated by cursorily glancing at the screen. If the quotation is long and must be read, you tend to lose touch with the audience.

Questions

Questions are powerful devices for capturing the attention of the audience. They can be used at any point in the presentation. The result is always the same: involvement of and participation from the audience. If a question/questions are used in the opening section of a presentation, they must be well thought out and related to the development of the case. The merit of using questions is that the presenter can get the audience into a thoughtful, active and participatory mode. However, there is a flip side to it as well. The members of the audience may get totally immersed in the question-answer session and leave little room for you to complete the prepared presentation. You, as a presenter, must be able to draw the audience back to the presentation if there are too many digressions or interruptions.

Questions can be rhetorical, meaning they do not solicit a response, or open, meaning a response is solicited. Both devices are useful, but require a different competency level on your part. In rhetorical questions, you can pose certain questions to the audience but not wait for an answer. These questions are normally floated in numbers of three. The purpose of using rhetorical questions is to get the audience into the thinking mode.

Example

> *In a presentation to the sales managers on increasing the sales target, the presenter can position the following three questions at the beginning of the presentation: Do you think you have achieved the highest target? Do you think you have fully realized your potential? Do you think your performance is at its peak?*

The audience is not provided with an opportunity to give a response. The presenter moves from the questions to the case being presented.

Open questions are those to which the presenter waits for the audience to respond.

'How do you think we can enhance diversity in the organization?'

Questions can be an effective tool for capturing the attention of the audience; however, the audience may become overly involved. When you ask a question and one member of the audience responds, other audience members may also be desirous of giving a response. If you are not adept at handling audience intervention, then the floor is totally lost. In a presentation of 30 minutes, the 2 and 2.5 minutes that you reserved for the opening may spill to 10 or 15 minutes. This can create problems since the time allocated to you is only 30 minutes. The entire structure of the presentation hinges on the time allocated. Even if you have a buffer of 5 minutes, it can be problematic trying to wrap up a case in much less time than one which is actually allocated.

Declaration

A declaration is a statement with a promise of value and truth to the audience. Used in the initial phase of a presentation, it can act as a very powerful device to get the audience hooked on to the presentation. It is unexpected and is frequently used by team leaders.

Our profits will increase by 30 per cent in the next financial year.

The credibility of the sender ascertains the acceptability of the declaration. If the same statement is made by a team member, the audience members will probably be skeptical and they will follow it up with many queries. However, if the declaration is made by the team leader, people are willing to accept the statement and eagerly await further substantiation of the point. When a declaration of this nature is made, a connection is at once established between the audience and the presenter. The audience is now agog, waiting for a response to when, why and how? As these questions are answered in the subsequent part of the presentation, attention is not lost throughout the presentation.

Though all these strategies are mostly used in the opening section of a presentation, many of them can also be used to boost a presentation and to get the audience back to life. Always keep these strategies up your sleeve. You never know when you may need to use a particular strategy. For example, in a very dry presentation, a presenter will be able to get the audience back to the fold by merely introducing a story from real life or from the Vedas.

Agenda

A traditional manner of beginning a presentation is to give the agenda to the audience and then follow it up. It is a stereotypical way of beginning a presentation but it helps in focusing on the key issues, the objectives and the conclusions. Many times the members of the audience do not have the time to spend in niceties. They want the details before they actually begin to listen to the presentation. In other words, they are looking for WIIFT. A response to WIIFT is the only method of forcing them to listen.

> The fifth commandment of structuring a presentation—
> *Remember the audience is on the search for VALUE
> in the presentation.*

Additionally, many organizations follow the pattern of giving the agenda as an organizational format for a presentation. Any deviations or creativity is not welcomed or accepted.

Example

> *After the introduction on the herbal skin cream to be launched, the presenter states, 'In today's presentation, we will be discussing the following points: The benefits of the herbal cream, its positioning in the market vis-à-vis other herbal creams currently available, the marketing strategy adopted for its launch, its distribution network and approximate sales figures we hope to reach within six months of its introduction.'*

It is during the planning stages that you decide which strategy will be most appropriate for the presentation. The decision is taken on the basis of the audience profile, their needs, the organizational culture and the time at hand.

Ideally, there should be a variation in the opening of a persuasive and informative presentation. For a persuasive presentation, the opening can be in the form of anecdote narration or scenario description, questions—rhetorical or open or any other strategy elaborated above. You can be creative in the choice of the opening. The same does not hold true of an informative presentation which is more in the nature of statement of facts and figures. In these cases, the beginning of a presentation can be in the form of statistical information, declaration or providing the agenda.

Note: **Make your presentation interesting by introducing anecdotes, humour, statistics, and the like.**

The Middle

The topic objective is to design content for informative and persuasive presentations.

The middle section or the body of a presentation comprises ideas or the main content. Issues are discussed and points established. The credibility of the presenter and the validity of the arguments are established in this section. The design and the content of this section is determined by the audience profile. For instance, a technical audience will appreciate points that are developed by a detailing of processes; for a non-technical audience, the processes are not important. The points or the issues under consideration become the focal point of concentration. Going again by the 30-minute presentation structure, you have almost 22 minutes to sell or present ideas and convince the audience of the authenticity of the presentation.

By virtue of difference in emphasis, the content development and presentation of both persuasive and informative presentation is different.

Content Development for Informative and Persuasive Presentations

In an informative presentation, information on rules, policies, figures, financials etc., are presented. In a persuasive presentation, the presenter makes an attempt to sell an idea or a product to the prospective customer—internal as well as external—or client.

While there is much information provided in an informative presentation, the sequencing is important. The presenter has to take a call on the structure to be adopted. Various methodologies for presenting content in an informative presentation can be: sequential, chronological, alphabetical, or spatial order.

Sequential refers to ordering of content in a definite, predetermined sequence. The sequence can be a result of patterning according to time or occurrence; chronological is in the order of time; alphabetical will refer to presentation of details according to alphabets, that is, if an annual review report is being presented, in all probability, the presenter will begin with administration and then move on to finance, HR, marketing, etc. A spatial ordering will be followed when description of a building, a machine or product is being made to the team. The description will follow a patterning in which you begin from one side or direction, say, top floor of the library, complete the description and then move to the middle and finally ground.

Example

If you are discussing the growth of the support system, you will present the details on the basis of the dates, chronology, or sequence of events. If you are presenting details on a machine, you will use the spatial order, that is, from left to right, clockwise to counter-clockwise, or reverse order. In a persuasive presentation, the sequence of ideas is not contingent upon chronology, but is based on the needs of the audience.

A persuasive presentation is need-based. Begin with the question: 'Why should or would the audience listen to my presentation?' Search for the answer. It can be as simple as

'Because they need the product or the services', or as complex as 'They may (probability) need the concept or the idea at a future stage.'

The former situation is easy to tackle as it is based in the here and the now. The second situation is tricky as you are unaware of the future needs of the audience, the market situation. You are making a sales pitch in the present so that it may reap its benefits in the future. For instance, a company may be planning a new facial cream in a couple of years and may be planning a merger with a FMCG. Your company is into manufacture of chemicals. Recently the R&D department has developed a chemical that enhances skin pigmentation. Many other companies are also in the process of research and development. You would like to announce that you are the pioneer in the product and all contracts at this stage will prove beneficial to both parties. You have inside information that the organization you are targeting is on the lookout for vendors. Making a sales pitch at this time will be advantageous as it would both publicize the product and help build relationships.

Both these types of presentations require careful planning and structuring. Use cue cards and prepare a logic tree to ascertain a logical structure and linkages between the points.

> The sixth commandment for structuring a presentation—*Develop content ensuring sequential arrangement of points.*

Example

You have to prepare a presentation called 'Enhancing Presentation Skills' for team members of the technical support staff. The stages in content development are given in Figure III.1.

Figure III.1: Stages in Content Development

a. Decide upon a topic, such as Presentation Skills.
b. Prepare a thesis, that is, a statement that sums up the objective of the presentation. Any topic would have many facets. All of them naturally cannot be covered. At this point, if you can zero down on the objective, the logic will automatically flow.
   Thesis: Essentials of a Good Presentation.
c. Write points, as they come to your mind, on separate cue cards. For example, the presentation can cover the following points:
   i. Voice Modulation
   ii. Visuals
   iii. Information Gathering
   iv. Pitch
   v. Font Size
   vi. Body Language
   vii. Font Style
d. Spread the cue cards on the table and categorize them according to content.
   For example, the points in the presentation can be categorized under Planning and Platform Behaviour. The Planning category can include Information Gathering. The Platform Behaviour category can include Voice Modulation, Body Language, and Visuals. You might include other points under these categories, if you like.
e. The remaining points on the cue cards that have not been categorized yet can be made subpoints.
   For example, Font Size and Style can be subpoints under Visuals and Pitch can be a subpoint under Voice Modulation.

> *The sculptor produces the beautiful statue by chipping away such parts of the marble block as are not needed—it is a process of elimination.*
>
> —Elbert Hubbard

Prepare a logic tree to ensure continuity and logic in the discussion. You will notice that while constructing the logic tree, many new points surface. The logic tree will in all probability look like the one given in Figure III.2 below.

Figure III.2: Logic Tree

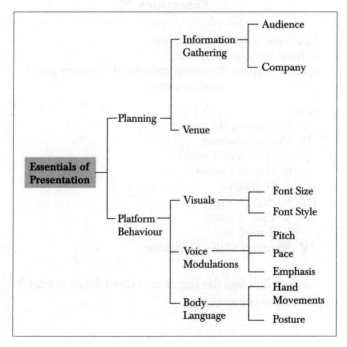

In the middle section, there is a difference in the structure of a persuasive and informative presentation. The difference is a result of different objectives of the two presentations. To elaborate, the focus of a persuasive presentation is on influencing or persuading the audience to a particular way of thinking and the focus of an informative presentation is to provide information to the audience members.

Figure III.3 lists the stages of content development for an informative presentation.

Figure III.3: Content Development for Informative Presentation

Title: New Model of a Computer
General Purpose: To inform
Specific Purpose: To inform the official members about the new system

Steps:
  I. Introducing the system
 II. Gaining attention
     a. How does it work?
     b. How is it better?
     c. Highlights
III. Special features
     a. Ease of usage
     b. Time-frame
 IV. Summary of the information

Figure III.4 lists the stages in content development for a persuasive presentation:

Figure III.4: Content Development for Persuasive Presentation

Title: Selling a Machine
General Purpose: To persuade
Specific Purpose: To persuade the client to buy the machine
Steps:
 I. Introducing oneself
 II. Introducing the product
 III. Gaining attention
  a. Benefits to the customer
  b. Work efficiency of the machine
  c. How is it better?
 IV. Highlighting special features
 V. Cost value
  a. How cheap is the machine?
  b. Comparative value
 VI. Warranty
 VII. Arriving at an agreement with the customer

A graphic representation of the points indicates a difference in emphasis. The focal points are different, and their development too is varied. It is interesting to note that the difference stems in the third section of gaining attention. Ideally, in an informative presentation, you familiarize the members of the audience with the product attributes. However, in a persuasive presentation, you highlight the benefits of the product. This difference stems directly from the objective of the presentation. While in the first case it is introduction of a product, in the second it is an attempt to sell the product. In other words, the difference emerges in the projection of points for gaining audience acceptance.

> The sixth commandment of structuring a presentation—
> *Use connectives and links to show continuity and flow.*

All ideas in a presentation are linked and the link must be specifically shown to the audience. The points or ideas cannot be presented in isolation. The points are linked with the use of transitives. Transitives are words that show continuity and maintain the flow.

Example

'In this presentation, we will present three points:
a. benefits of the product;
b. financial implications; and
c. future course of action. There are a number of benefits of the product...'

It is interesting to note that in this example, the presenter at the beginning of the discussion informs the audience that 'three' points will be presented. This information is followed by a detailed description of the points. Prior to the commencement of each point words like 'first', 'second', 'third' or 'a', 'b', 'c' are used, which are also referred to as transitives. This strategy helps maintain continuity, and keeps the members of the audience well-informed on the development of the points. For instance, in the above example, you describe the benefits of the product and then follow it by a statement: 'The second point to be discussed is the financial implications.' In this statement, 'second' is a transitive. It indicates to the audience that the first point is over and a discussion over the second point is about to begin. Transitives keep the audience engaged as you move from one point to another. Apart from numbers, other transitives include 'next', 'following from the previous point', 'to add', 'further', 'additionally', 'therefore', and the like.

Just a Minute! **Have you decided which transitives to use?**

> The seventh commandment for structuring a presentation—*Understand the difference in objective between an informative and persuasive presentation and then begin the process of structuring.*

The End/Closing

The topic objective is to make an impressive closing to the presentation.

The end or closing is nearly as important as the beginning. While the beginning compels the audience to listen to the presentation, the end, if forceful, reverberates in the mind of the audience and forces them to reflect.

There are various strategies to end/close a presentation. The choice is contingent on your objective. If it is an informative presentation, then you have no choice but to reiterate the points that have been made in the course of the presentation. However, if it is a persuasive presentation, it can close on a note of call for action. Whichever be the case, the end must necessarily be emphatic, reiterating the points that were raised in the course of the presentation.

The various techniques/strategies for closing a presentation are as follows:

- Return to the theme of the opening statement
- Challenge

- Call for action/motivate
- Recapitulate the main points

Return to the Theme of the Opening Statement

A presentation has a theme, a purpose or an objective which is stated by most presenters, in the opening sequence. In the closing sequence you may decide to come full-circle and end on the same note on which the presentation was begun. As a strategy, this method of closing is effective as it reiterates the purpose or objective of the presentation.

Example

If the presentation's objective or purpose is to provide information on a new software installation procedure, the presenter can close with the following statement: 'We come to a close of our presentation, in which we tried to explain the basic procedures involved in installation of the software.'

Challenge

Motivation garbed as a challenge is a device frequently used by team leaders. If a difficult request is made, in all probability employees start with resistance. However, if the request is posed as a challenge, all are motivated to accept the challenge and perform to the best of their abilities.

Example

Suppose you are a senior product manager presenting information on the challenges faced by the company due to increasing sales of the competition and the actions that must be taken. You can close your presentation on the following note: 'We have taken a look at the challenges we face, we need to put in extra time, effort, and energy to combat the same. Can we, as a team, rise to the occasion and enhance our performance?'

If you notice in this particular instance, three strategies merge in this closing sequence: *challenge, motivation,* and *appeal for action.*

Call for Action/Motivating

A presenter who is at a higher level than the audience members can use motivation or call for action as a device for closing the presentation. Such a line of presenting moves the audience from just logical or rational thinking to a feeling of ownership. This approach is especially useful when the presenter is making demands on the audience.

The audience has to be coaxed, cajoled and persuaded into taking up something out of the ordinary, going one step beyond what is required of them. If the monetary or tangible benefits of such an initiative are low, then the feeling of an emotional and moral responsibility has to be stirred so that the company's goals become *their* goals.

Creating a sense of ownership and pride in their work enhances their ability to take on more work and yields better results.

Example

You are heading the team of technical staff in the production department. You have described the reasons for changing the existing system and provided the details. However, to bring about this change, your team members must make more contributions without additional compensation. Currently you are not aware of the resources that will be provided to you by the organization. In the closing, you will make an attempt to motivate the audience and make a call for action. 'We need to put in extra effort. It is our department and the growth of the department is our growth. Let us all put on our thinking hats and decide on the best possible strategy for implementing the change. We will meet in a couple of days and decide on the most suitable strategy.'

Recapitulation of Main Points

In the closing section, the presenter summarizes the main points for the audience.

The main reason behind the summary or recapitulation is that while the presenter is familiar with the content of the presentation, the audience is not. Hence, what may seem logical and easy to understand for the presenter, may not be as simple for the members of the audience.

Also, attention span of most human beings is quite low and there are very good chances that

> *The wise ones fashioned speech with their thought, sifting it as grain is sifted through a sieve.*
>
> —Buddha

you would have 'lost' the members of your audience at some point or the other during the presentation. Summarizing helps the audience members fill the gaps that they may have missed out because of their inattentiveness.

Overall, recapitulation also helps reinforce what you want to convey and thus brings more focus to the key issues.

Example

In a presentation that contains the following points, developed over a period of 30 minutes,

o *Benefits of the machine*
o *Costs involved (Installation and maintenance) Rs 15,000*
o *Approximate number of X-rays being done in a year by models of X-ray machines currently in use*
o *Distribution and degree of usage across departments*

You will close in the following manner:
'Today we discussed the benefits of the machine, the installation and maintenance costs which came to Rs 15,000...'

A conclusion is a summation of the content addressed. New ideas cannot be introduced in the closing sequence. There are certain statements referred to as problem statements that must be avoided in the presentation 'Did I mention that . . .', 'We had the same problem, by the way, last year when . . . ', 'Oh, another thing I should have mentioned . . .' Statements of this nature or akin to the ones stated above indicate lack of planning, and clarity. The audience does not view these statements very positively.

The closing section of the informative and persuasive presentations are different. If you are making an informative presentation, restate the main points or summarize the presentation in the closing. In a persuasive presentation, you can use motivation, appeal for action, or challenge as a strategy depending on what is the objective of the presentation. If you decide to reiterate your points as a strategy for closing, then sum up the points made in the course of the presentation.

Note: **Start and end your presentation on a positive note.**

Let us look at the difference in the structure of an informative and persuasive presentation. Table III.5 differentiates between the steps to structure an informative presentation and a persuasive one.

Table III.4: Structuring a Presentation—Informative and Persuasive

	Informative	*Persuasive*
Planning	• Collate all information and gather information about the audience. • Prepare the agenda.	• Collate all information and gather information about the audience. • Select the Unique Selling Proposition.
Presentation The Beginning/ Opening	• Give statistical information (should be crisp!) • Narrate an incident that helps build the information, e.g., Information on a new product to be launched, Efforts made by R&D personnel to	• Move in the audience's camp and address the issue from their point of view (You've got them hooked!) • Start with rhetorical questions (You've got them from the passive to the active state)

(Contd.)

Table III.4 (*Contd.*)

	discover the product despite all odds. • Give the agenda.	• Start with open questions (You've got them to participate, but they might take the floor from you!) • Start with a story/scenario description…, e.g., 'Reminds me of a story…' or 'Once upon a time…' or 'In today's newspaper…' or 'If you remember two years back…'
The Middle	Proceed by: • Topical development • Chronological order	Proceed by: • Indicating understanding of the audience, rousing their emotions, and giving reason and logic.
The End /Closing	• Restate the main points • Summarize the entire presentation	• Reiterate appeal to emotions and needs • Challenge • Motivate

The eighth commandment for structuring a presentation—*Close the presentation keeping the main objective in sight.*

Presentation Boosters

The objective here is to describe strategies that enhance a presentation.

By now, you have done your rehearsals and are confident that the presentation will be a value add for the members of the audience. Unfortunately, when facing the audience you realize that the audience is getting restless or bored. You have probably not been able to get them to reach the same level of enthusiasm as you experienced, or your assessment of their needs is at fault. There appears a mismatch between the expectations of the audience and the presentation. One of the many reasons can be the time or 'when' the presentation is made. For example, your presentation comes at the end of the day and the audience is tired and restless. Additionally, it may happen that there are other high priority issues on the mind of the audience members at the time of the presentation.

To ensure concentration and attention of the audience and reduce boredom, use the following presentation boosters:

- Make the presentation interactive
- Make use of pronouns/names
- Narrate an incident
- Use examples
- Provide statistics
- Use visual imagery

Make the Presentation Interactive

Statistics prove that the best method of assuring retention of the presentation, in the minds of the audience, is to get them involved. The higher the involvement, the greater

the recall. Make the presentation interactive and participative. Throw questions at the audience, get them to respond, wait till you elicit their response or interest. You
can also ask for opinions on the points being raised. The
key to success lies in making the audience feel that their
opinion is of utmost importance to you. No sooner do you
sense that there is a group which has either tuned off or is
getting restless, make an endeavour to address your points
or questions directly at them. Open-ended questions can
be raised. Definitely some extra time will be spent in the
application of this strategy and you may have to reduce
the content to be able to meet the time-line. In this situation, a choice will have to be made between presentation
of dense content and presentation to an alert group. Most
presenters would like to go in for the second option.

Example

> *In a presentation by a visiting faculty to the students of
> an operations research class the teacher can ask the
> students, 'What are your expectations from this ses-
> sion? What is your objective in attending this session?'*

Make Use of Pronouns/Names

In a presentation situation, the presenter is an alien by
virtue of the role assigned. All members in the audience
are closely knit by virtue of the purpose for their presence
or being members of the same team or department or
organization. It is the duty of the presenter to bond with
the audience members. The sooner it is done the easier it
is to proceed and gain acceptance. When you as the presenter arrive at the venue, and are unfamiliar with the audience members, make an effort to find out the names of

the group members. Addressing them by their first name in the course of the presentation helps in bonding. In almost all presentation scenarios there are tent cards in front of the members. In the initial phase concentrate on a few names, and memorize those names. These names should be of people sitting across the room and not in one corner. You can pick up one from the left, one from the right and one from the centre. The purpose of selecting these names across the room is that it gives the group a feeling that you are concentrating on all and not just one section of the group. While raising questions or discussing use these names. You will realize that in the first five minutes of your presentation you have been able to learn/memorize three to four names. Repeat the strategy, concentrating on other names. The effort will not go unnoticed.

Additionally use of pronouns, like 'you' and 'we' also help in bonding with the audience members. They feel that the presenter is one of their group members, hence the acceptance is easier. You become one with the audience when the pronoun 'we' is used. 'You' addresses the audience directly and helps in soliciting their attention. However excessive use is to be avoided as it can have a negative impact on the audience.

Example

You must have noticed that in your 15 years of work experience . . .

The ninth commandment of structuring a presentation—
Devise methods of making the presentation interesting and appealing.

Narrate an Incident

Always keep a few stories/anecdotes/incidents handy while making a presentation. Narrating an incident in the middle of the presentation is a powerful technique. Judging the appropriateness of the incident is important. If you can narrate an incident with which the audience is familiar or can relate to, the attention will be higher than usual. For instance, a column of the newspapers on 20 September carries the following news item: 'the discovery of chemical "Mauve", by company X after repeated trials has proved successful in curing cancer. A 100 people have responded favourably to the chemical.' Store this information in your memory. If you have to make a presentation to the team members on a new project to be undertaken and you need to motivate them, talk about this chemical and how after repeated trials, it became successful. If the audience can relate to the incident, chances of success are high.

Example

If you are part of the market research division of an automobile company and are presenting information on the feasibility of introducing a new car, you can give an illustration of situations in which an increase in the income levels of the middle class, leads to higher purchasing power and incentive for purchase of new vehicles.

'Today when the purchasing power of the middle class is on the rise, and the market conditions are ripe, it is time for us to introduce the new car so that there is high acceptability.'

Use Examples

Examples bring to life the concepts presented. A general complaint for the failure of many presentations is that the members of the audience are not able to relate to the ideas that are being discussed. Use examples from real life and those that are close to the audience. If you are making a presentation on leaders, use examples like Gandhi, Vivekanand, Subhash Chandra Bose, Krishna and Arjuna. If you begin discussing leaders like Napolean and Hitler, it may be difficult for the audience to relate.

One of the advantages of using examples is that the audience is able to remember and recall points when explained with the help of examples. It is difficult for the audience to remember all the points made during a presentation. However, it is easy to remember the examples. At a later stage, if they can place the examples in the right perspective, it will be easy to remember the points by association.

Example

In a presentation to the support staff for a BPO company, examples from other such BPOs must be used. The audience will be able to correlate and remember the points.

Provide Statistics

Numbers/statistics can be provided either in the opening or in the middle of the presentation. In the corporate world, much hinges on the accurate use of numbers. Only those statistics must be provided which would hold the attention. Excessive use can lead to an information over-load. It is difficult to remember all numbers. If you decide to display numbers, slides are not an appropriate device. Handouts can be prepared and you can, in the course of the presentation give the handouts, pause for a couple of minutes, let the members absorb the numbers and then carry on with the presentation.

The advantage of giving a few numbers on the screen and many in the handout is that in the former case the audience does not get confused with numbers and the attempt to memorize them or mentally work them out. In the latter case, the audience can carry the handouts with them and need not make an attempt to memorize. Use of numbers and their analysis usually impresses clients. In any business, the merit or value of a presentation lies in the amount of homework done by the presenter.

Example

Provide the financials—the figures that will capture the attention of the corporate houses. Show numbers but not too many.

Note: Check and recheck to ensure that you are ready with all the supporting aids.

Use Visual Imagery

Visual imagery has the power to stimulate the senses and capture the attention of the audience. The choice of words should be such that the audience begins to feel, see or hear. Abstract or concrete nouns make the text dense and heavy and occasionally make the presentation sound pedantic. Visual imagery makes the presentation alive and appealing. If through use of visual imagery, you can stimulate the senses of the audience, then they are sure to remember the point being made.

Example

> *If you are part of the administrative team and are presenting information to doctors about the plight of patients, the following statement can be made: 'The patients in the wards are not very comfortable as we do not have sufficient staff to attend to them. By the time the nurses come, the patients suffer in the ward.'*

Contrast this statement with the following statement:

Example

> *'The patients lie in the wards with blood oozing out of their wounds and staining the bandages. We need to increase the number of staff/nurses so as to be able to provide immediate attention to the patient.'*

In the second statement, the visual imagery captures the attention of the audience. While the implicit meaning in both utterances is the same, that is, we must increase the number of staff in the hospital, the impact of the second is greater because of the use of visual imagery.

> The tenth commandment for structuring a presentation—*Prepare the presentation boosters in advance and use them as and when the need arises.*

Checklist

Do's	Don'ts
Sequence and structure the presentation	Leave the presentation unstructured
Build credibility in the eyes of the audience	Sound incompetent or unknowledgeable
Assess the capability of the audience	Over/under estimate the capability of the audience
Be clear in your thought processes	Rush through the structuring of the presentation
Develop the content based on the capability of the audience	Develop the content based on your own knowledge/capability
Use facts and figures to capture the attention of the audience	Use facts and figures merely to show knowledge
Be consistent in approach to the topic and the content	Bring in a variety of approaches
Provide the agenda at the beginning of the presentation to keep the audience focused	Begin a presentation without giving proper thought to the structure
Make declarations as a different strategy to open a presentation	Make the presentation openings boring and monotonous
Hook the audience to the presentation by the use of anecdote narration or scenario description	Leave the interest factor in a presentation unattended
Use appropriate humour/jokes to enliven the atmosphere	Use humour/jokes which only appeal to you
Work extensively on the opening and the closing	Leave the opening and closing of a presentation unstructured
Structure the middle keeping the objective in mind	Prepare the content of the presentation without being sure of the needs of the audience
Adopt a variety of strategies to keep the interest of the audience high	Be insensitive to audience demands in the course of the presentation

SUMMARY

1. Work on the 7 Cs
2. Be credible as a presenter
3. Ascertain the context
4. Develop the content
5. Ensure clarity
6. Keep all channels open
7. Be consistent in development of points
8. Assess the capabilities of the audience
9. Spend extra time on developing the opening
10. Develop the closing based on the development of the main content.
11. Make use of transitives to emphasize and maintain flow and continuity
12. Use presentation boosters to retain the interest of the audience
13. Keep a few presentation boosters up your sleeve to be used in moments of stress and crisis situations

Chapter IV

Creating Visual Aids (VAs)

Create your own visual style... let it be unique for yourself and yet identifiable for others.

—Orson Welles

Like all forms of design, visual design is about problem solving, not about personal preference or unsupported opinion.

—Bob Baxley

Designer

OBJECTIVES

- ❑ Identify methods of enhancing a presentation
- ❑ Select the criteria for scripting content on the visuals
- ❑ Prepare a checklist of VAs to be used
- ❑ Select the criteria for choice of VAs
- ❑ Determine the most suitable VA for your Presentation

Key Words	
Bar Chart	Pie Chart
Charts	Single Line Graph
Cue Cards	Six-by-Six Rule
Double or Multiple Line Graph	Stacked Bar Chart
Floating Wedge	Tables
Flow Chart	TECT
Organizational Chart	Visuals
Pictograms	Visual Aids

INTRODUCTION

Are you creative? Have you ever stopped to give an advertisement or a hoarding a second look? Paused and wondered at the creative inputs that have gone into making the advertisement or hoarding worth a second glance? Think, what is so extraordinarily special about these visual modes of communication that force you to take a second look and marvel at the design and the content? You can be sure of one truth, almost a commandment for designing the visual—thought, effort, creativity and time (TECT) is required for creating a visual. TECT ensures visual and mass appeal, which, in turn, aid long-term retention.

Creating VAs for presentations hinge on similar principles as are applicable for any graphic representation used for marketing or advertisements. VAs are slides that are pictorial or schematic representations/illustrations of data, points, graphs, and charts that help in explaining concepts and ideas and can be prepared on transparencies, if the medium of projection is an Overhead Projector (OHP) or in the form of slides for a PowerPoint presentation. They can also be in the form of movie clips to illustrate a point.

VAs are extremely effective devices for making successful presentations if you are clear of their usage and are equally certain about the content to be used. Let us assume that you have structured the content of the presentation and are raring to give it a shot on the slide. Wait! Do not rush through the process. Think analytically, dispassionately and objectively. Can the entire content to be delivered in the course of the presentation be listed or punched on the computer in the form of slides? Definitely not! Careful thinking and prudent pruning of the text is to follow a meticulous and proper designing and structuring of the content. An interesting research reveals that when a person listens, his/her retention rate is around 20 per cent. However, when visuals are presented along with the information, retention rates can shoot up to 50 per cent. Thus, if the message is to be remembered, VAs are to be used with caution. Hence, the need for application of TECT.

A simple rule for the design and structure of VAs is: ensure creativity and clarity in the design and the content of the slides. In the process of making the slide creative, do not lose sight of the link between the design and the content. Definitely, if the VA is pictorial, the message is meaningful and retention is high. For example, if you use the rupee sign to represent the inflation rate in the country, the VA becomes a value add to the presentation because the audience is able to see the link between the sign on screen and the verbal content. Creativity and clarity in the design gently persuade the audience to new ways of thinking.

VAs are used for the following reasons:

- To attract the attention of the audience

- To impress the audience with clarity, specificity, and precision of points
- To clarify ideas
- To simplify concepts
- To emphasize points
- To summarize the main ideas

The first commandment for creating visuals—*Ensure the use of TECT.*

In this chapter, you will learn the following aspects of creating visual aids for a presentation:

- Content
- Steps in Planning Content of the Visuals
- Designing VAs
- Pictorial Description on VAs
- Types of VAs
  - Slides for PowerPoint
  - Transparencies
  - Black and White Board
  - Flip Charts
  - Movie Clips

Content

The topic objective is to determine the criteria for information on the slides.

You have already structured the content to be delivered, now begins the process of structuring the content for the slides. This step is half completed when the sequence of the main content is decided. The task ahead is to now decide which points are of prime importance and need to be displayed on screen and which are supplementary or secondary and can be discussed as appendages to the main points without being flashed on the screen. The major difference between an oral presentation that does not make use of slides and a visual presentation is that in the former case, examples and anecdotes are used for elaboration of ideas and in the latter, only ideas are scripted.

Some questions that come to mind are: How is the amalgamation between the two types of presentations to be brought about? How is information to be used/presented? The information on the visuals is to be used as a beginning point for discussion and elaboration. Examples and anecdotes are used to exemplify the points and extend them from a conceptual plane to an application zone.

Example

In a presentation on the principles of communication you decide to discuss the concepts of cooperation, turn-taking and politeness. Your slide may be simple with three points and may read as follows:

Exhibit 1

Principles of Communication
1. *Cooperative Principle (Grice)*
2. *Turn-taking System (Schegloff)*
3. *Politeness Principle (Leech)*

This is a simple slide with minimum content—but will the audience be able to remember the principles or the names of the researchers who proposed these principles? Additionally, is the audience interested in the concepts or the application of the concepts?

Suppose you begin on the following note: 'Have you ever seen a case of communication in which there was no cooperation from one party, no politeness on either side, with one participant speaking and forcing the other to listen? It can, by stretch of definition, be defined as communication, but definitely not effective communication. The situation can be made effective if the three principles of communication, namely, cooperative, turn-taking and politeness were to be followed. How, is the question we now need to address . . .'

When planning your information, ask yourself the following questions:

- ❑ Will the points add value if they were displayed on the screen?
- ❑ Why must I put only these points and not other points on the slide?
- ❑ Do the points match the objective of the presentation?
- ❑ Am I giving the right amount of information to the audience by using these points, or am I cluttering my slides with too much information?

Information must be sorted into groups that can be used for slides. For example, if you are making a presentation on the attrition in the company, sort the information into groups like: attrition in other companies, causes for attrition in your company, global situation, salary structure in the market, what can be done to prevent attrition. You now have five major pockets in which the rest of the information must be grouped. If you notice, in this particular case, we have not spelled out the objective of the presentation. It can be to provide information on the attrition rate in the company to the HR department or it can be to persuade the top management to change policies to minimize the rate of attrition. With a change in the objective, there will be a change in the design of the content of the slides.

> *Good design, at least part of the time, includes the criterion of being direct in relation to the problem at hand—not obscure, trendy, or stylish. A new language, visual or verbal, must be couched in a language that is already understood.*
>
> —Ivan Chermayeff

Example

The purpose of your presentation is to emphasize the salient features of a new software. Information that can be provided is as follows:

- *Financial implications of the software*
- *Benefits to the corporate world*
- *Comparative study of the new product with existing software*
- *Strategies for converting data into information*
- *Analysis of process for analysing, communicating and sharing results*
- *Development of data solutions*

Begin by providing an answer to the above mentioned questions. Will explication of all these points add value if displayed on screen? No it would not, as the focus is on emphasis of salient features of a new software. You would end up providing redundant information.

Which points must I display on the screen and which must I ignore? Only those points must be used which add to the development of the main story line of the presentation, which in this case is 'salient features of a new software.'

Do all the points listed in this example match the objective of the presentation? No, they do not. Some are redundant as they provide information which is outside the purview of the discussion agenda.

Does the information match the expectations of the audience, am I giving the right amount of information to the audience by using these points or am I cluttering my slides with too much information? The question on the right type of information again must be answered keeping the audience and presentation perspective in mind. In this particular example, enumerating all the six points is an information overload. The audience is left trying to figure out 'why this surfeit of information?' While it is good to sound knowledgeable, cluttering a presentation with too much information is not the right method of displaying knowledge.

Now that you have considered all these questions, you will realize that if you concentrate on all these points and project all of them, the focus is lost. Consider deleting the first three points and concentrating on only the last three. You will find that the presentation has gained in substance and is now more objective oriented.

The second commandment for creating visuals—*Select criteria for presenting content on visuals which should in all cases be familiarity with the overall objective of the presentation and audience expectations.*

Steps in Planning Content for the Visuals

Topic objective is to develop VAs to supplement the content.

Now that we are sure of the criteria for deciding the content, we now need to begin the process of planning the steps and strategies for designing the content.

The five steps for planning content for the VAs are:

- Collating raw data on cue cards/computer
- Sifting through and analysing the information
- Visualizing the points
- Aligning visuals with verbal or oral components
- Avoiding information overload on slides

Collating Raw Data on Cue Cards Computer

In the previous two chapters you have learned the merits of collating raw data on cue cards. The advantage of working with cue cards is that it is much simpler rearranging the cards than cutting and pasting on the computer. This is not a commandment, but merely a suggestion for designing the content. If you feel comfortable with the computer, go ahead. Use the computer to punch in the points and cut and paste for a logical sequence. Identify the medium or strategy with which you feel most comfortable. The logic behind using cue cards is that it is a much simpler process and can be worked on at any place. The choice of course is that of the presenter.

The first step in planning content for the VAs is to collate raw material on the cue cards or the computer.

Sifting through and Analysing the Information

The raw material for the design of the VAs is collected. The next step is to sift through the information, delete the unnecessary or redundant information and analyse the information with you. Clear all webs of doubt in your mind, logically study the analysis. Clarity in your mind will lend itself to clarity in content design, lack of which will prove to be an information overload for the audience.

Example

You have been asked to make a presentation on the costs involved in running a chain of hospitals across the country in the last three years to the top management. The data you have collated is as follows:

Year	Costs	Profits
2003	Rs 500,000,00	Rs 50,000,00
2002	Rs 450,000,00	Rs 45,000,00
2001	Rs 400,000,00	Rs 40,000,00

If you are unsure of how to use this information, you may as well delete the information. However, if you analyse this information there are some interesting conclusions that can be derived. If these conclusions match with the overall objective of the presentation, and the audience expectations, your task is half accomplished.

Analysis of the raw data reveals that:

1. *Every year there has been an increase in the costs by Rs 50,000,00.*
2. *Correspondingly there has been an increase in the profits by Rs 5,000,00.*
3. *There is a direct relationship between costs and profits.*

4. *The more you spend on infrastructural support the greater are the chances of making profits.*
5. *The steady increase in the costs by Rs 50,000,00 will make it easy to make future projections.*

In this particular example, the overall objective of the presentation is to provide the top management with the information on the costs involved in running a hospital and the audience expectations focus on the analysis of the information. Both these criteria are met and chances of your success in this particular case seem to be high..

The third commandment for creating visuals—*Analyse the facts and state the analysis on the slides.*

The next step is to list the possibilities from this analysis and take a decision and chalk out a course of action most suited to the development of the presentation.

Exhibit 2

Future Course of Action

- **Recall all Wonderpack from market**

- **R&D Activity**
  - **Change contents to suit climatic condition**
  - **Extensive tests to be done**
  - **Different products for different skins**

Arvind Gupta & Mahesh Gupta

Let us analyse the information presented on this slide. While spelling out the future course of action, only 'R&D Activity' has been specified. Under which department would the activity of recalling the product ideally fall? Marketing? This means that the slide should have two main points 'Marketing Activity' and 'R&D Activity'. Let us now examine the subpoints under R&D Activity. While the 'Change contents to suit climatic condition' and 'Extensive tests to be done' are appropriately clubbed, the third subpoint is a cause for concern. Stating it as 'Different products for different skins' does not make it a R&D Activity. If the point was reworded as 'Create different products for different skins', it would automatically fit the bill or be part of the cluster.

The problem in the above slide would not have arisen, if the presenter would have carefully analysed the information, before using it on the slide.

Note: Analyse the information before presenting it on the slides.

Visualizing the Points

Begin the process of visualization. Which points can be most appropriately displayed on the screen and which cannot? Which points must be graphically represented and which can go as simple and plain text? For instance, if you are presenting sales growth, or showing a comparison between any two variables or projecting figures, you can go ahead with graphics or charts and tables. However, if your concern is primarily presentation of points, then a text format is the most suitable. Suppose you wanted to project your analysis on screen, you may decide to use figures and text. Exercise caution! In your enthusiasm to present details you may decide to clutter slides with too much information which may be difficult for the audience to either grasp or retain. If you feel that there is too much content on the slides and is proving to be a hindrance, request a friend to read and grasp the points. Time the process. If it takes over 30 seconds, then it is information overload. Use the visuals sparingly. Ensure that visuals are used only when there is a need and necessity and you feel that they add value and not detract from the main body of the oral content. Make use of graphs and charts to simplify rather than complicate issues.

> *Visual appearance is one of the most effective variables for quickly differentiating one application from another.*
>
> —Bob Baxley
> Designer

If you have information that cannot be presented in the time allotted, then, prepare handouts. Do not distribute them before or during the presentation. It is a natural tendency for members of the audience to flip through and read the handouts while a presentation is being made. Losing out on the audience attention in the initial phases of the presentation is not a very good strategy with which to begin your presentation. However, there may be instances when you provide a handout during the course of the presentation.

Example

If you are explaining certain financials to the audience, it may be difficult to project all of them on the screen. Try giving the audience a single page handout and explain the details provided on the page.

In this example, you have conducted a market analysis and have come up with certain findings. The findings can be presented on screen and the process of analysis on a one page handout. As the findings are discussed you can draw the attention of the audience to the process of the analysis on the handout.

> ***Just a Minute!* Have you carefully thought of the reasons for using a particular type of visual aid?**

Aligning Visuals with Verbal or Oral Components

The purpose of using slides is to reinforce the message; and to act as a memory jogger to the oral message. Their purpose is to remind you of the points in the presentation, the points on which you can and need to elaborate. In case you forget a certain point a glance at the slide helps recollect the point, galvanizes the thinking process and you are once again in control of the situation. Illustrations, pictorial representations, graphs and charts, and text visuals can all be used on the slides for reinforcing the message and acting as a memory jogger.

The fourth commandment for creating visuals—*Create visuals that reinforce the message and act as a memory jogger.*

Exhibit 3

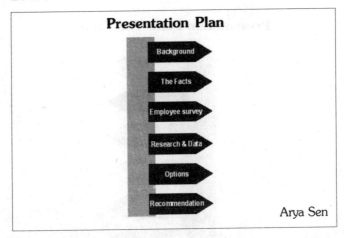

This is an interesting and creative way of presenting the agenda on the slide. The audience is informed at the beginning of the presentation what is to follow and what to expect.

Exhibit 4

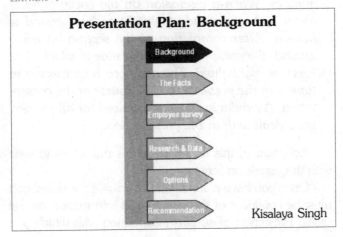

Exhibit 5

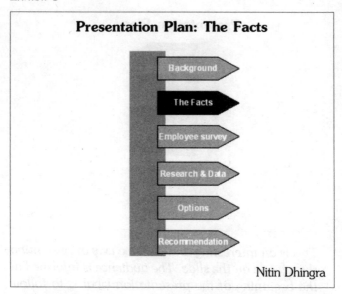

Presentation Plan: The Facts

Background

The Facts

Employee survey

Research & Data

Options

Recommendation

Nitin Dhingra

In these two slides, the presenter keeps the audience abreast with what is to be discussed in the next few minutes. When a discussion on the background is about to begin a slide highlighting background is flashed. After completion of the section on background, the presenter shows the slide in which 'The Facts' is highlighted. The audience is constantly in tune with the presenter on the course of the presentation. A similar strategy is followed for all the sections dealt with in the presentation.

Adoption of this technique keeps the words in sync with the visuals on screen.

Once you have planned and structured the slides, you must be confident of the quantum of information on the slides. Projection of surplus information with which you are not comfortable, can create problems. Let us assume you have done your research and have come up with a good analysis. You decide to project the same on the screen. Obviously it is difficult to memorize all the information, so you read through the text on the slides. Contact with the audience is lost as you turn your back to read through the slides. If planning is thorough and points carefully presented, a glance at the screen is sufficient for continuing the presentation. Too much time must not be spent reading the content on the slides. A cursory glance of approximately fifteen seconds is sufficient before you launch into an explanation. This raises another important issue of planning. How much content can be put on the slides?

Look at the following two slides:

Exhibit 6

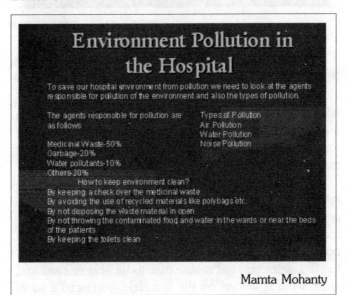

Exhibit 7

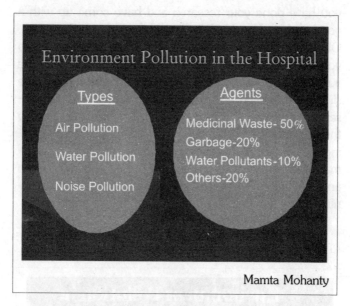

Which slide captures your attention? First or second? Without doubt, the second. Why?

Let us try and analyse the reason. The first slide contains too much disorganized content. If you notice there are many running sentences which take much more time for the reader to grasp than simple points each containing not more than five to six words.

Contrast this slide with the second slide which contains less content, which is well thought out, properly sequenced and arranged and can be read at a glance. Remember TECT? Additionally, the second slide has few points, each point containing two words. If you begin reading the slides you will realize that to be able to read and grasp what is written on the first slide, you need a minimum of 40 to 50 seconds whereas, in the second slide 10 to 15 seconds are sufficient to grasp and comprehend. Which then, is preferable? The answer is not far to seek. Whatever is comfortable for you will also be comfortable for the audience.

> ***Note:* Use minimum content for maximum gain**

Avoiding Information Overload on Slides

In the previous section we briefly touched upon the merits of avoiding information overload on the slides. While in theory it is acceptable and recommended, what is the rule for application of the concept?

The golden rule for planning slides is a six-by six rule, i.e., each slide must contain a maximum of six points, each containing no more than six words. The points must necessarily follow one another and the link between them be established by the presenter. Let us assume that we are talking about influence strategies. The main objective of the presentation is to provide the audience with the information on influence strategies. You can restrict yourself to two slides which contain information on:

— Hard strategies
— Soft strategies

Collate all the tactics that come to your mind. Do not begin categorizing them. Once you are through with the listing, you can begin clustering them under different heads. Let us assume that you have come up with five tactics, namely, aggression, assertiveness, ingratiation, bargaining, exchange.

Decide, based on your understanding of the literature on influence, which tactic will fall under which category. Under the first category, you can club all the tactics that define hard strategy, that is, aggression, bargaining, and assertiveness. On the second slide you then position tactics that fall under the category of soft tactics, namely, exchange, and ingratiation. When in the process of designing the presentation do not confuse between the major and the minor points. The connect, the link in the development of the points will be lost. If you can stick to the storyline, or the main objective of the presentation, continuity and clarity are maintained adding consistency to the presentation.

Note: **Follow the six-by-six rule**

Enthusiasm is good . . . but a presentation is not the place to be overenthusiastic. In your enthusiasm to present all points, you may create an information overload for the audience. Try to match the level of your slides to the level of understanding and sophistication of the audience.

Exhibit 8

Our Marketing Strategy

Place – Tapping Rural Markets
- 600000 villages in India.
- 25% of villages in the 5 states of Karnataka, Kerala, Maharashtra, Andhra Pradesh and Tamil Nadu.
- These account for 65% of the total rural population i.e. approx 700 million population – a very large market.

Nakul Tewari & Neha Bhargava

Let us analyse the above slide. In the enthusiasm to present data, there has been a mix of information. The place, obviously cannot be 'Tapping rural markets' this, naturally, has to be a strategy. Let us now examine the three points presented on the slide. The first provides information on the number of villages in India, the second on the states where one-fourth of the villages are located and the third, information on the percentage and number of the population size. If you carefully glance through these three points you will realize that none of them are actually strategies for tapping rural markets. They are all part of a long paragraph from which the connecting words and clauses have been removed. The paragraph would probably read like this:

'There are 600,000 villages in India. Twenty-five per cent of villages are in the five states of Karnataka, Kerala, Maharashtra, Andhra Pradesh and Tamil Nadu. These account for 65 per cent of the total rural population, i.e., approx. 700 million population—a very large market.'

This is an informative slide presenting details on the number and percentage of villages in India, where they are situated and the population inhabiting them. The dichotomy between the title of the slide and the information presented as content for the slide proves to be an information mismatch and overload for the audience.

The fifth commandment for creating visuals—*Avoid information over- or under-load.*

Exhibit 9

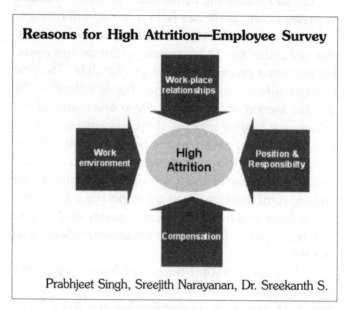

Reasons for High Attrition—Employee Survey

Work-place relationships

Work environment

High Attrition

Position & Responsibilty

Compensation

Prabhjeet Singh, Sreejith Narayanan, Dr. Sreekanth S.

Information overload can be avoided by designing slides as presented above. Four major points leading to high attrition in the organization are presented. Animation can be used in this presentation where one point appears on the screen after another. It gives the presenter time to explain and the audience time to grasp.

Planning the number of slides is equally important. Imagine you are in the process of designing a 30 minute presentation. How many slides can you use? Ten or 20? Hypothetically, the number sounds good as you have so much content and to be able to do justice to all the content you think you definitely need that number of slides. But have you ever wondered what will be the plight of the poor recipients? Do you actually think that they will be able to grasp the content on all the slides and be able to retain the message? If yes, then you ARE an optimist.

Let us try working out the logical implications of using too many slides.

In a 30-minute presentation you spend two minutes for the introduction, one minute for conclusion and five minutes for questions and answers. You are left with 22 minutes to present the content. Even if you have 22 points (sub points) you will need 22 minutes to explain the points. If each slide contains six points, ideally you are talking about one slide in six minutes. Hence going by logic you can use only three and a half to four slides. If you are very good at designing slides and want to show off your expertise to the audience or have to show a process in operation, add a couple of extra slides for effect. Net usage of slides in a 30-minute presentation should not exceed six slides.

Warning! **Do not clutter the slide with too much information.**

Designing VAs

Topic objective is to design VAs with minimum content and maximum visual appeal.

Once the planning for the content on the VAs is complete, the process of designing them begins. Keep the following factors in mind when you commence the designing process.

Necessity of the Visuals

Only use visuals to add to the content or enhance the presentation. Necessity is based on the needs of the audience.

Example

During a presentation on the financial implications of the development of new software, a statement can be made that is self explanatory: 'Costs incurred are tremendous.' However, it is not sufficient. You need to elaborate on the costs incurred and why you feel they are huge or tremendous. Elaborate on the statement with the help of visuals. Indicate the costs on screen, show comparative figures of previous years or justify your statement with the help of visuals.

In this particular example, if you decide to use visuals for explication of a point, you and your need is totally justified. You will notice that in this case your needs match with those of the audience which makes the use of visuals if not mandatory then definitely essential.

Exhibit 10

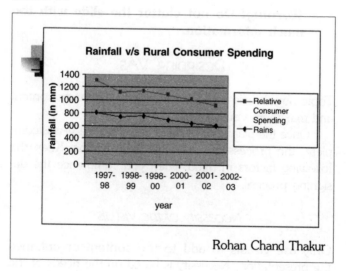

Let us assume that you need to use a line diagram to show rainfall v/s consumer spending. You have given the process some thought and have come up with a design for it. Before you display this slide, glance through it again. Does it meet the requirements of the audience? Definitely not! No matter who is your audience, this graph is a waste of time. In the year 2005 if you decide to present data as old as 2003, it loses its significance. The audience always needs current information. Presenting only backdated information is a waste of time, energy and resources.

In this example, the presenter has only invested in terms of ECT, that is, effort, creativity and time. No thought has been given to the process. This then is a case of gross information 'underload' where redundant and outdated information is presented.

> The sixth commandment for creating visuals—*Use a visual to present correct and well thought out information.*

Accuracy and True Presentation of Details

Is the slide accurate and truthful? If a graph is to be used, ensure that all data is accurately represented.

Example

You wish to show the sales figures of the last five years in two different regions, east and west. There is a major overlap in terms of sales representation and you want to graphically represent it with the use of a line graph.

Careful! The points of intersection or areas where there is an overlap must be accurately represented. Errors on a slide are unacceptable. The audience will absorb all that is visually represented, which further reinforces the results of the presentation. If there is a difference between what you say and what you show, the audience will find it difficult to assimilate. When in doubt, consult an expert for guidance or avoid presenting charts and graphs altogether.

A good way of checking the design and the content of the slides is to imagine there is someone sitting at the end of the room. Ask yourself the following questions before you begin with the design of the visuals:

- Are the visual large enough for the person sitting right at the back to see?
- Are the designs simple enough for comprehension?
- Can the audience members read the words used on the slides?
- Which format of the slides conveys information accurately and truthfully—horizontal or vertical?

Exhibit 11

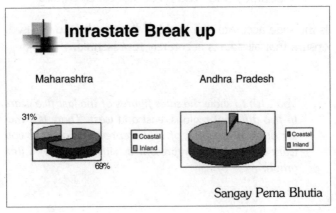

Let us consider the following example. Two pie charts have been presented showing coastal and inland break up of two states, namely, Maharashtra and Andhra Pradesh.

If you take a careful look at the pie-charts you will realize that aesthetically they do not appeal. One box and the pie within the box are smaller than the other. While this error is pardonable, the second is absolutely unpardonable. No numbers are presented in the pie chart for Andhra Pradesh. The percentage is left to the imagination of the viewer. It could be 10 or 5 per cent for coastal and 90 or 95 per cent for inland. The slide lacks in accuracy and true presentation of details.

Warning! **Inaccurate or incomplete information can mislead or disinterest the audience.**

Pictorial Description on VAs

Topic objective is to use various types of charts and graphs to depict information visually.

It is best to use simple graphs and charts that 'tell' rather than confuse. The selection of different types of charts or graphs is based on the need and the necessity of presenting a specific type of presentation. Follow the six-point formula to keep visual aids simple.

Data can be represented by using different forms of charts and graphs (see Table IV.1).

> *It is more important to do the Right Thing than to do the Thing Right!*
>
> —Peter F. Drucker

Table IV.1: Types of Charts and Graphs and their Uses

	Charts and Graphs	*Uses*
1.	Tables	To present uncomplicated, specific data.
2.	Single Line Graphs	To plot growth or show a trend.
3.	Double or Multiple Line Graphs	To show a comparison between trends or growth over a period of time.
4.	Bar Charts	To show quantity.
5.	Stacked bar Charts	To show multitudes of data.
6.	Pictograms	To represent data in the form of symbols.
7.	Pie Charts	To represent percentages in the form of a circle.
8.	Flow Charts	To show relationships between processes, procedures, and concepts.
9.	Organizational Charts	To represent various units, hierarchy, and channels in the organization.

Tables

Tables are representations of specific data. When you need to provide details that are uncomplicated but essential to the development of the presentation, use a table. In a table, columns and rows contain the facts and figures. In other words, a summary of the findings is given in a tabular form.

Example

You have been asked to present the statistics for Ward 1, Ward 2, and Ward 3. A tabular form will be most suited for this kind of presentation, as it provides simple and uncomplicated information at a glance.

Exhibit 12

Statistics for Wards 1, 2 and 3

	January	February	March
Ward 1	10	15	25
Ward 2	11	23	20
Ward 3	20	15	20

Single Line Graph

Line graphs are used to plot growth or show a trend. There are two axis—x and y. The X axis is the horizontal line and the Y axis is the vertical line. Two variables, like time and growth rate are selected and the relationship between the two is projected. On the X axis, the time zone is provided and on the Y axis, growth in terms of sales is projected. The relationship between the two, either in the form of an incline, plateau, or decline is represented on the graph. An ***incline*** is represented by a vertical line, not necessarily straight, beginning from the X axis. A ***plateau*** is a horizontal line on the graph, indicating stability. A ***decline*** is represented on the graph by a vertical line which drops on the X axis.

Exhibit 13: Single Line Graph

Exhibit 13 shows a company's profit margin growth during the past five years. The profit margin between 1997–98 was .2. In 1999, it increased to .7. However, in 1999–2000 it declined to .4. There is sharp increase from 2000 and in 2001. The profit margin reached 1. From 2001 to 2002, the margins remain constant, representing a plateau. As the profit margin drops in 2002– 03, the graph shows a slant. Depending on the increase,

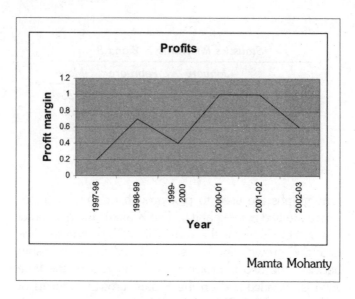

Mamta Mohanty

decline, and stagnancy of the profit margin, the graph shows peaks, crests, troughs, and plateau, respectively.

The seventh commandment for creating visuals—*Use a graph or chart that can truly represent your data.*

Double or Multiple Line Graph

Double or multiple line graphs are comparative graphs that show trends or growth over a period of time. If you are comparing two trends, then plot two lines on the same graph to show their relationship. Two lines can intersect or overlap indicating a similarity in the trend or growth pattern, which helps the audience understand the concept. However, you must be careful while plotting lines. Too many can clutter the graph and make the slide unreadable. Try not to exceed beyond three lines on a single graph.

Exhibit 14: Double Line Graph

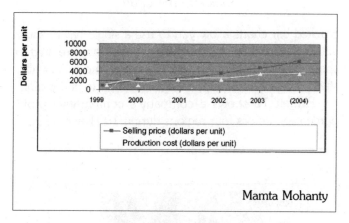

Bar Chart

A bar chart consists of bars projected vertically to show quantities, such as costs. These charts are most commonly used in presentations and are the easiest to produce and create maximum impact.

Exhibit 15: Bar Chart

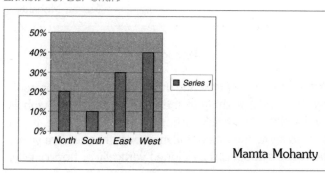

Exhibit 15 shows the percentage increase in profits for the four regions of a company.

Stacked Bar Chart

Stacked bar charts allow you to use a single bar to show data for more than one category of data. They are used to show the relationship of parts to the whole. Visually, stacked bar charts are appealing and simple to understand.

Exhibit 16 shows a company's comparative profit percentage across four regions during 1991 and 1992.

Exhibit 16: Stacked Bar Chart

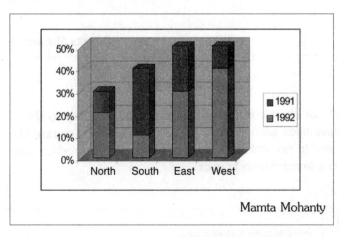

Mamta Mohanty

Pictogram

Pictograms are creative and innovative ways of representing data and the study in the form of symbols. Symbols can be plotted vertically or horizontally on the slide. If you want to show the rate of inflation over the past five years, the rupee symbol can be plotted vertically or horizontally.

Exhibit 17: Pictogram

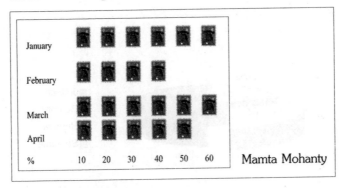

Exhibit 17 shows the number of telephones installed from January–April.

Pie Chart

A pie chart represents percentages and is plotted in the form of a circle. Slices of a pie are used to represent percentages. When using a pie chart, use a ***floating wedge,*** which is similar to a slice of pie detached from the whole. The slice attracts the attention of the audience and helps build on a point.

Exhibit 18: Pie Chart with a Floating Wedge

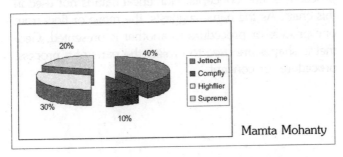

Exhibit 18: Pie Chart

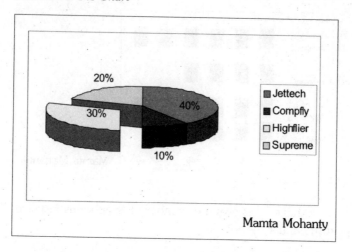

Mamta Mohanty

The figures above show the market share of four hypothetical companies. While discussing the market share of all four companies, use Exhibit 17. For discussing the market share of one particular company, use Exhibit 18.

Flow Chart

The flow chart shows the relationship between processes, procedures, and concepts. Numerical data is not used in this chart. As the name suggests, the move or flow from one process or procedure to another is presented. Geometric shapes are used to project the parts of a process, procedure, or concept.

Exhibit 19: Flow chart

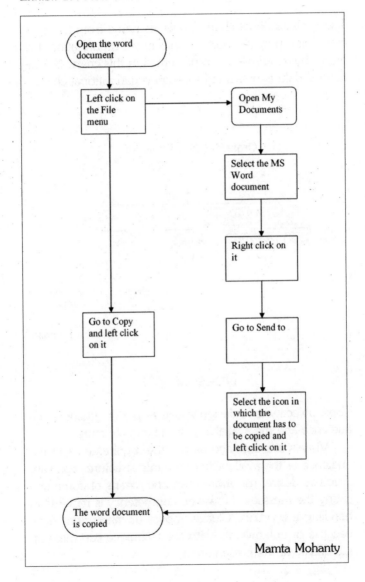

Organizational Chart

The organizational chart derives its name from the concept that it projects. Various units in the organization, the hierarchy, channels are represented in this chart. No numerical data is presented through organizational charts.

**Exhibit 20: Organizational Chart

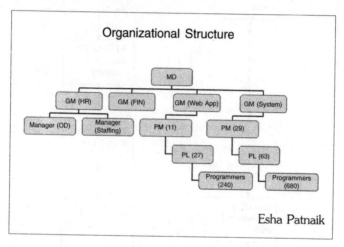

Types of VAs

Topic objective is to design visuals as per the needs of the audience and the availability of the infrastructure.

Visuals are designed as per the requirements of the audience or the availability of the infrastructure. You can, if you so desire, use more than one means of communicating the message. However, competency is required in handling the visuals. Clumsy moves or inadvertent slips, because of unfamiliarity with the technique can mess up the quality of the presentation.

Tips for Presenting Visuals

- Show a visual only when you are ready for discussion. Follow the display by a discussion on the points.
- Remove the visual after you have finished discussing the point.
- Do not leave the projector on; put it on the standby position. This brings the attention of the audience back to you. However, it takes approximately 30 seconds for the projector to get activated from the standby position. You must plan your speech keeping this 30-second lag in mind.
- Practice using the visuals to prevent last minute hitches.
- Carry additional floppies that contain a copy of the text. To play it safe, mail a copy of the presentation to yourself or to the organizers a couple of days in advance.

Slides for PowerPoint

Designing slides for the presentation is perhaps one of the simplest techniques available. We refer to it as the simplest because of the ease with which the computer can be used to learn and then design, define and animate.

The only problem that can be envisioned at the time of using the computer is the font size and the font style. What looks readable at a close distance may seem unreadable when viewed from the back of a room. As far as possible use pastel colours that soothe the eye. Too bright or too dull colours may mar the impact of the slide.

Adhering to the principles discussed above, use Serif or Arial font style. The font size for the text should be anywhere between 34 and 36. The title however can be slightly larger and you can follow 36, 38 or 42 size. The title can be written in capitals but the rest of the text must necessarily be in regular font. All lights in the room need to be dimmed for the right effect.

Once the text has been composed on the computer, it will need to be copied on a floppy, CD or a memory stick. Always carry additional floppies or CDs or copy the data on to a floppy, memory stick and a CD. Many times, especially when you are travelling abroad, the computer configuration may be different and you may not be able to use the floppy/CD/memory stick. A still safer technique for very important presentations is to mail the copy of your presentation in advance to the concerned party with a request to load it on their system. Other techniques to be used to play it safe are: mail a copy of the presentation to your account and take a printout of your presentation. You can always get it Xeroxed and circulated to the participants so that they are with you at the time of delivering the speech.

The eighth commandment for creating visuals—*Check the font size and style from a distance to ensure readability.*

Just a Minute! **Have you tested the slides for readability and colour combination?**

Transparencies

Though outmoded, transparencies are still followed at some places as the medium for presenting the information visually to the audience. Text on the transparencies needs to be written in advance. Use a ruled paper beneath the transparency, so that the lines you write are straight. Neatness definitely adds value to the presentation. The ruled paper is not the ordinary ruled paper used in copies. The lines on this paper are wide apart and make it easy to write with a large handwriting.

The title on the transparency should not begin right at the top. Leave a horizontal margin of at least 2 inches on top and at the bottom. The text should be written in such a manner that the transparency, once placed on the OHP, does not have to be moved. You can use a pencil as a pointer on the transparency, which will get reflected onto the screen. But if you are nervous please do not use a pencil to point as the tremor in the hand gets magnified and displayed on screen.

Practice with the transparency is extremely important. Inadvertently, speakers place it upside down. Many a times the audience has to point out the flaw and then begins the ungainly attempt at correcting the error.

> ***Warning!*** **Practice using the transparencies to avoid error of logistics at the time of presentation.**

The best colour to use on a transparency is black which reflects very well and has the desired impact.

On many occasions the speakers decide to use more than one type of VA to communicate the message. One of them is of course the PowerPoint presentation which is prepared and the other could be a flip chart, a transparency or the black/white board. The speaker writes down all the comments of the audience members on the transparency and keeps it aside in the 'parking lot' and digs it up at the end of the presentation to show that all points or all queries raised by the audience have been efficiently attended.

> The ninth commandment for creating visuals—*Do not leave unattended the questions and the observations in the 'parking lot'.*

Black and White Board

The black and the white boards are the most traditional methods used for teaching or presenting. They are the easiest to handle and no preparation is required. They are ideal for teaching through cases. As the audience keeps presenting their views and comments the facilitator can keep jotting them down on the blackboard and with the help of arrows build a connection between the various viewpoints discussed in the session.

Black and white boards can also be used with a slide show. The presenter can move to the board either in the midst of the presentation or at the end of the presentation and jot down points presented by the audience members. Black/white board then becomes a 'parking lot' for storing information to be handled at the end of the presentation. To ensure readability, all lights, especially the light over the board should be switched on.

You have to be careful of your handwriting when writing on the board. It should neither be too small nor too large. Practice writing in capitals. It improves readability. In fact, you can, in the practice session, write a sentence in regular handwriting and then repeat the sentence in capitals. Go to the end of the room and view for yourself. An objective analysis will tell you which writing style to adopt. Writing in capitals will definitely slow down your pace of writing, but it is a very small price that you will pay for ensuring readability.

Note: Use a combination of visual aids for varied impact.

Flip Charts

Flip charts are always kept handy when there are no black/white boards. They are used as a substitute for the traditional blackboard. They are kept ready and handy to be used in case there are comments raised by the audience members which cannot be addressed at that point in time or there are diagrams that need to be drawn on the spur of the moment to explain a concept.

Almost the same principles as explicated for the black/white board are used.

Movie Clips

Movie clips are an interesting means of presenting ideas and concepts. You drag the audience from their passive state and get them interested in the points being presented.

A movie clip can show a process, or be part of cinema. What is important while showing movie clips is that they should not exceed three or five minutes and should ideally be followed by a discussion. If the movie clip is too long the audience may drift off, making it difficult for you to get them back to the mode of listening to the presentation.

The tenth commandment for creating visuals—*Use movie clips of only two or three minutes*.

Selection of movie clips is crucial and must be done on the basis of the level of the audience and the needs from the presentation. Movie clips when combined with power point slides make the presentation very effective, provided the presenter knows how to handle the two modes of communication efficiently.

> ***Warning!* Unnecessary or unrelated movie clips detract rather than add to the impact of the presentation.**

Checklist for Creating Visuals

Do's	*Don'ts*
Follow TECT	Be impulsive in creating visuals
Ensure clarity and creativity	Provide inaccurate or incomplete information
Clarify and simplify ideas	Use complicated graphs and charts
Emphasize relevant points	Emphasize redundant information
	Clutter the slides with too much information
Determine the criteria for information on the slides	Create slides without first identifying the reason for the visual
Form clusters of points	Present 'underload' of information
Visualize the points	Use running sentences
Align Visuals with Verbal or Oral Components	Present the entire oral component on slides
Analyze the information	Fidget or jump slides
Follow the six-by-six rule	Use long movie clips for entertainment

Design VAs with minimum content and maximum visual appeal	Use too much of animation
Use a variety of VAs	Be monotonous in choice of VAs

SUMMARY

1. Invest in TECT: Thought, Effort, Creativity and Time.
2. Ascertain the reason for choice of VAs which could be to attract the attention of the audience, to impress with the clarity, specificity, and precision of points, to clarify ideas, to simplify concepts, to emphasize points or to summarize the main ideas.
3. Sort information to be used on slides into groups or clusters.
4. Identify the primary and the secondary points.
5. Develop VAs that supplement the content.
6. Research and analyse the information before presenting it on screen.
7. Remember the purpose of slides: to reinforce the message or act as a memory jogger.
8. Follow the six-by-six rule for good content structure on the visuals.
9. Plan the number of slides—do not 'overload' or 'underload' the audience members with information.
10. Select the most appropriate diagram or chart on the basis of your content.
11. Represent the content pictorially or graphically in the form of a table, a bar chart, a stacked bar chart,

a line graph, a double or multiple line graph, a pie chart, a pictogram, flow chart, or organizational chart.

12. Follow a readable font size and style.

13. Play it safe. Always make arrangements for alternate methods of visual display for cases of emergency.

14. Select from the different types of VAs: slides for power point, transparencies, black and white board, flip charts, movie clips.

15. Use a variety and combination of VAs to attract the attention of the audience.

EXERCISE

Caselet for Oral Presentation

Presenters: General Manager, Marketing, Mumbai and his team members

Audience: Chairman and Vice President (Marketing), General Manger (R&D), HXL, Mumbai.

Objective: To provide information on sale of a new cream, Wonderpack, in the rural market.

Background: In a recent advertisement, HXL made tall claims about a cream to be launched in the market. They stressed that the presence of the chemical P2O, much talked about in western countries, reduced pigmentation and brought a glow to the complexion. Its continuous use for six weeks would, without fail, improve the texture of the skin as well as enhance looks. The R&D and marketing division, after elaborate discussions, decided to first experiment it in the rural market before launching it in the urban sector. After six months the sales team got back with very negative reports. The cream did not prove to be a 'wonder cream'. In fact, P2O did not suit the climatic conditions of India. Application of the cream produced rashes on the face, which subsided only after taking steroids. The cream had been shunned in the rural market and the name of the company was being sullied and all its products boycotted by the people.

The suggested pattern for slides is as follows. The following slides were prepared by the following students: Hitanshu Gandhi, Shraddha Vohra, Mansur Nazimuddin, Vipin Agarwal, Jatin Didwania.

Remember you can be still more creative and come up with a host of other ways in which you wish to proceed. This is just a sample and will be of help to those venturing into the area of designing visuals for the first time.

WonderPack
- Sales and lessons

Marketing Division
HXL Inc.

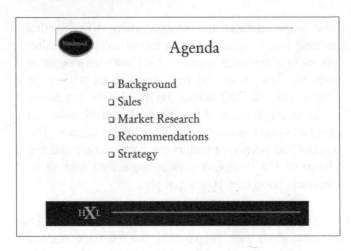

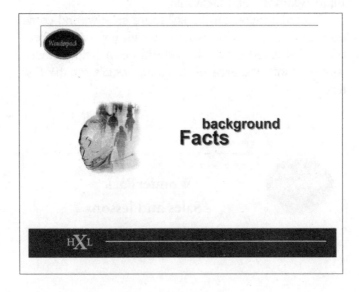

WonderPack: The Brand

Agenda
Background
Sales
Market Research
Recommendations
Strategy
Profile

□ #1 fairness cream worldwide:

◦ First launched in 2003.
◦ Exclusively marketed in US, Europe.
◦ Commands 75% of the segment.

□ Active ingredient: P2O, exclusive to HXL

H**X**L

WonderPack: Marketing Mix

Agenda
Background
Sales
Market Research
Recommendations
Strategy
Profile

□ Product: Premium advanced fairness cream
□ Price: Slight premium over Pond's
□ Promotion: Schools, colleges, radio spots, direct sales
□ Place: Rural Maharashtra

H**X**L

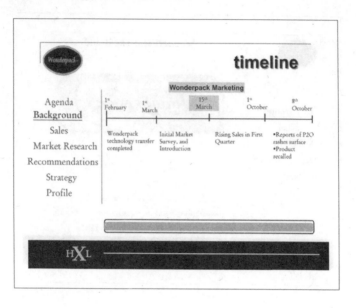

Sales

Agenda
Background
Sales
Market Research
Recommendations
Strategy
Profile

- ❑ **Rationale behind selection of rural market of State of Maharashtra**
  - ❑ Demographics
  - ❑ Income distribution

- ❑ **Established Company Image**
  - ❑ Distribution Network

Market Share of Fairness Creams

Agenda
Background
Sales
Market Research
Recommendations
Strategy
Profile

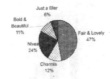

- ❑ Based on survey conducted by internal team
- ❑ Survey caters to rural market of State of Maharashtra
- ❑ Survey results compiled on the basis of data gathered from retailers and distributors in the region

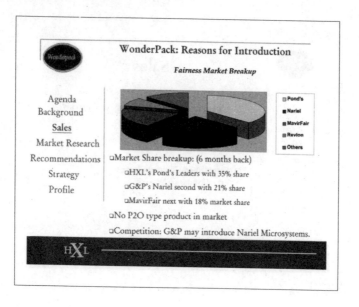

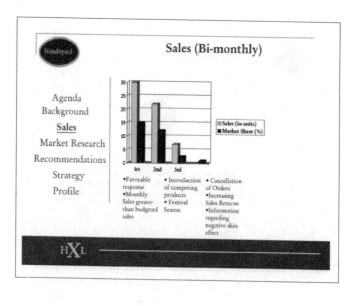

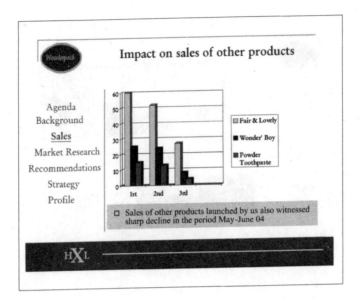

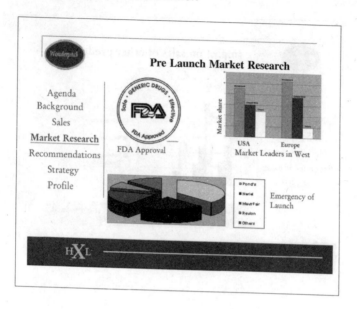

Pre Launch Market Research

Agenda
Background
Sales
Market Research
Recommendations
Strategy
Profile

FDA Approval

USA   Europe
Market Leaders in West

Emergency of Launch

HXL

Post Launch Market Research

Agenda
Background
Sales
Market Research
Recommendations
Strategy
Profile

❑WonderPack target market:

 ❑Customer profile (age, literacy, sex etc)

 ❑Customer buying behavior (word of mouth publicity, Product perception)

 ❑Environment/External Factors (Marriage Season and rains , over-application as is a sunscreen, steel packaging in hot climate)

HXL

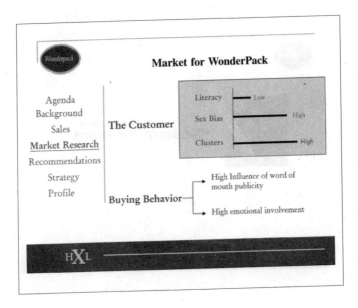

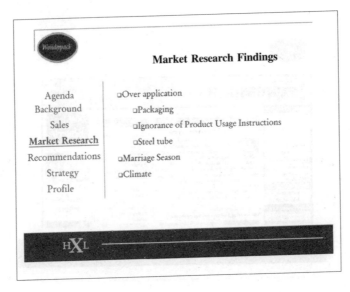

Short – term
Recommendations

HXL

PHASE I – Quick Fix

Agenda
Background
Sales
Market Research
<u>Recommendations</u>
Strategy

- **Issue a Press Statement**
  - Accept Responsibility
  - Apologize
  - Assure quick action
- **Warn against further use of product**
- **Recall WonderPack from the market**

PHASE II – Comeback

Agenda
Background
Sales
Market Research
<u>Recommendations</u>
Strategy

- **Advertising Blitz**
  - Company Image
  - Emphasis on Trust
- **Send product for extensive R&D testing**
- **Re-packaging**

OUR CREDO

Agenda
Background
Sales
Market Research
Recommendations
<u>Strategy</u>

•Maintaining Values
•Ethical Conduct
•Sensitivity to customer needs
•Building Trust

LOOKING AHEAD...

Agenda
Background
Sales
Market Research
Recommendations
<u>Strategy</u>

- Crisis Management Team
- More stringent quality measures
- Follow-up Information Processes

H**X**L

LOOKING AHEAD...

Agenda
Background
Sales
Market Research
Recommendations
<u>Strategy</u>

"It will take time, it will take money, and it will be very difficult; but we consider it a moral imperative, as well as good business, to restore Tylenol to it's preeminent position."

James E. Burke
Chairman, Johnson & Johnson

H**X**L

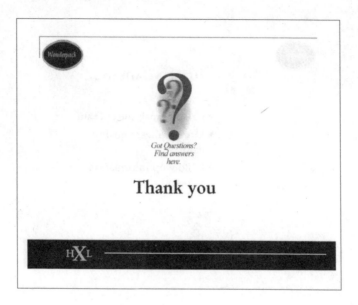

Chapter V

Delivering a Presentation

Oral delivery aims at persuasion and making the listener believe they are converted. Few persons are capable of being convinced; the majority allow themselves to be persuaded.

—Johann Wolfgang von Goethe
German Poet

Before speaking, consider the interpretation of your words as well as their intent.

—Andrew Alden

OBJECTIVES

- ❑ Identify methods of exercising control
- ❑ Determine objective of the presentation
- ❑ Establish control over the self
- ❑ Identify audience preferences
- ❑ Develop techniques for effective handling of situations

Key Words	
Adapt	Gaze
Additions	Humour
Address	Nerves
Agreements	Objections
Body sport	Parking Lot
Credibility	Question answers
Disagreements	Rehearse
Disruptions	Voice articulation

INTRODUCTION

How many times have you stood in front of the mirror and thought, 'This is MY time. I will make it and make it big this time. Will I succeed? What will happen if I make a laughing stock of myself?' Relax, not only you but almost everyone faces a similar apprehension before making a presentation, be it to a small or a large group. If the size of the group is too small, say, four or five people, problems faced are different from those when encountering a group of say, 50 or 60 people. The best size (not always in your control) of the group is 20 or 25 individuals.

While the content of your presentation is important, it is not always a case of what you say but how you say that strikes the chord and gets the audience to listen attentively to the presentation. You may have done a lot of research and come up with many concepts, but if the concepts, content and the text are not understood by the audience, the purpose is defeated and the time spent in research and analysis is wasted.

There are times unfortunately, when the manner in which we present detracts from the desired effect of the presentation. Sometimes, very rarely though, the content is so powerful that the manner of presentation becomes insignificant. For instance, as the head of the organization, if you announce a raise of 10 per cent, or as the head of an academic institution you announce an unexpected break for a week, the audience does not really care about what you do with the techniques of delivering a presentation. The content in itself is so rich and audience-centric, that it overshadows all other essentials.

In other situations, it may happen that the presenter is so powerful in the delivery, that the content takes a back seat. The audience is enamoured by the walk and the talk and is willing to forfeit concentration on the text. But this again is a rare phenomenon and does not happen all the time.

There may be a third situation in which the presenter is able to bond totally with the audience right from the start. This may be because of personal contacts, initial interaction, responses to queries or status of the presenter. The audience is willing to forgive and forget errors, if any, in the course of the presentation. The presenter is in complete sway over the emotions of the audience.

All three instances cited above are rare. As ordinary presenters aspiring to achieve an accomplished status, we need to be able to exercise control over all three aspects—the material/content, the audience and the self.

The first commandment for delivering a presentation—*exercise control over MAS—material, audience and self*.

View the process of delivering a presentation as a game—of exercising control—over the material, the self and the audience. It is advisable to be in control over all three in the initial phase before you create a niche for yourself and are accepted as an ace presenter, with skills and qualities not easily replicated.

The process for exercising control is broken into three categories:

- Exercising control over material
- Exercising control over self
  - Nerves
  - Body language
  - Voice modulations
- Exercising control over audience
  - Handling audience interventions
  - Answering audience questions

Exercising Control over Material

Topic objective is to determine criterion for sequential arrangement of material.

The material/content for the presentation has been structured (see Chapter III). How do you now exercise control over it?

Yes, the material has been planned and structured but finally, before the delivery, check the objectives of the presentation once more to ensure that all criteria for this event are successfully met and the interest of the audience can be sustained.

Just a Minute: **Have you rechecked the objective of making a presentation?**

The objective of the presentation can be to:

- Inform
- Persuade

- Motivate to action
- Sell
- Teach
- Train

Let us assume that you are working in the R&D department of a pharmaceutical company and have prepared a presentation on a new drug, 'Megapix', to cure AIDS. The product is to be launched by your company in a month. Let us see how with a change in the objective the focus of the presentation and the manner of presenting will also change.

To inform: As a manager in the corporate communications department, you may be asked to do an informative presentation to the media representatives on the new drug. In this scenario you will present the composition of 'Megapix', the potency, benefits and side-effects, if any.

To persuade: As the manager, marketing, you may be asked to do a persuasive presentation to probably distributors, retailers and sales representatives. You will begin by talking of the benefits of 'Megapix', its comparison with other similar drugs in the market and the long-term benefits associated with the company.

Motivate to action: As the team leader, R&D department, you may be asked to motivate the marketing division people to promote the drug, 'Megapix', on which they have little confidence. You can begin the presentation by a discussion of the merits of 'Megapix', how proper sales can boost the market share of the company, how proper promotion can help the company create a niche for itself in the domestic and international market.

To sell: As a medical sales representative, you may be asked to convince the doctors to prescribe the medicine to the patients. In a face-to-face presentation, you may begin your talk by showing the product and the literature and substantiating it by providing additional information on the merits of the drug and the process through which the authenticity of the drug was tested in the laboratory.

To teach: As the head of the R&D department, you have been asked by the top management to instruct the fresh recruits of the department on the processes of the division. You could use the example of 'Megapix' in your methodology. In the presentation, you will present multiple perspectives, ways of approaching a problem and methods of deriving a solution. You will use the example of 'Megapix' to demonstrate the multiple runs over subjects before claims of success can be incorporated in the promotion of the product.

To train: As head of the training department, you may be asked to train the members of the marketing division to make presentations on the new drug, 'Megapix'. You will need to discuss strategies for making informative and persuasive presentations (discussed in chapter II), using 'Megapix' as an example.

You will notice that with a shift in the objective, the focus of the presentation has also undergone a change. To keep the attention of the audience hooked on to the presentation, examine and reexamine the objective, to ensure interest, ascertain that your focus matches with that of the audience.

A speech should be like a woman's skirt: Long enough
to cover the topic yet short enough to be interesting.

—Winston Churchill

Exercising Control over Self

Topic objective is to exercise control over self.

The game is about to begin ... have you all your cards
in place? Do you have time to practice? For any game you
play, practice and still more practice helps in perfecting
the strokes and increasing the probability of success. It is a
similar case with presentations. If you aspire to succeed in
the game of making presentations, rehearse and then rehearse some more—the guru mantra for success.

The second commandment (guru mantra) for delivering
a presentation—*Rehearse, rehearse and rehearse!*

Rehearsals are an effective way of exercising control
over the self. Practice in front of a mirror. The mirror tells
no lies. If you are objective and critical, you will be able to
identify errors, if any, in the style of speaking or body
language. So far, you may have assumed that you look
very confident, have a perfect smile and gesticulate the
right way. However, when you stand in front of the mirror
and speak, the first thought that strikes your mind—'Gosh
can it really be me? I look awful!' The 'look' in this case
does not relate to the natural looks with which we all are
endowed. 'Look' in this case refers to your movements,
the way you smile and the manner in which you gesticulate. Can something be done? Yes, if you are critical and

are willing to accept changes, much can be done to restore your image in first your own eyes and then in the eyes of the audience members.

Note: **Practice makes perfect.**

Nerves

Have you ever stood in front of a large audience and felt the gentle or violent tremor in the knees, a churning in the stomach and a flush on the face? Don't worry. You are not the only one who has faced this problem. Believe me, almost anyone who says that the audience does not create fear in the pit of the stomach, is untruthful. 'I'm getting butterflies in my stomach. What should I do?' 'I have forgotten all that I was supposed to be presenting!' 'I can't stand up. My knees are shaking!' and similar statements are often heard from presenters on the verge of facing the audience. Don't panic; it is natural and normal to be nervous. It helps in good preparation and better delivery. Knowing that you possess the potential of getting nervous before a presentation will force you to be meticulous in your preparation.

Let us begin by understanding the curve of nervousness before we look for remedies or solutions to combat the shortcoming. Nervousness during the presentation or jittery feelings take on a very steep incline that lasts only for a couple of minutes after which it is a plateau stage. In other words, nervousness at the beginning of the presentation increases for a couple of minutes after which it stops and does not increase any further. If these initial few minutes are controlled at the time of delivery, the rest is easy … for the journey to success has already begun.

Warning! **Do not let nervousness bog you down. It is NATURAL to be nervous.**

Theoretically and conceptually it is easy to say, 'Well in a few minutes after beginning the presentation you will be fine, so relax and face the audience!' There are some strategies that can be followed to quell the nervousness in the initial few minutes. The first thing to do before beginning application of any of these strategies is to understand the feeling of nervousness in the pit of the stomach. It is only when you recognize this emotion that you will try strategies to relax the taut muscles. Don't ever suppress the feelings of nervousness. The more you suppress, the more will they erupt with volcanic force. Let the feelings surface and come up. Recognize the statement 'Yes I am nervous'. The moment you realize the nervousness, it has escaped from the pit of the stomach and is now perched like a demon on your shoulder. It is so much easier for you now to throw the demon off your shoulder. See Table V.1 for more strategies to control those nerves.

Just a Minute: **Have you been able to identify the nervousness in the pit of the stomach?**

Table V.1: Strategies for Controlling Nerves

1.	Breathe deeply
2.	Drink warm tea or coffee before the presentation
3.	Eat something light before the presentation
4.	Give yourself a pep talk
5.	Imagine that the audience does not know anything

Begin the process of throwing the demon off your shoulder by breathing deeply. Put your hand on your stomach and follow the balloon mechanism. When you breathe in, the stomach must come out and when you breathe out, the stomach must go in. Sounds strange, but begin practicing and you will find it does wonders to the system.

When you are nervous there is a rush of adrenalin which makes the throat dry and parched. Drink tea and coffee with sugar before the presentation. Water, aerated drinks or anything cold must be avoided. Tea and coffee are stimulants and contain a necessary amount of caffeine to give you the desired stimulation and instant intake of sugar makes the insulin in the blood level shoot up giving you the desired stamina

Always eat something light before the presentation. Preferably biscuits rich in glucose content. The 'butterflies in the stomach' feeling gets quelled and you are physically at rest and in a position to deliver the presentation.

Warning! **Do not go on stage on an empty stomach.**

You have tried all the strategies and find that none of them works and your knees are still unable to support you. Go to the rest room and give yourself pep talk. 'I'm good are'nt I? I'll succeed, won't I? What's there to stop me from succeeding?' Boost your morale and your confidence and step out as a changed and confident you.

The third commandment for delivering a presentation—
Let not the fear eat the self, let the self eat the fear.

You have tried all the strategies and are still nervous. Adopt this last technique—without doubt it will help you restore your balance. Imagine that the audience has donkeys' ears growing out of them—the audience does not know a thing and you are the expert and will provide expert details and comments on the issue under discussion. Remember, this technique is to be followed only in extreme cases. The moment you begin to feel that the audience is good for nothing and knows little, the attitude also changes. It becomes condescending and disrespect-

ful and gets translated in the voice and manner in which questions are tackled. The audience is wise enough to understand this approach. Their response to your presentation then is equally condescending and disrespectful.

> *Do the thing you fear to do and keep on doing it ...that is the quickest and surest way ever yet discovered to conquer fear.*
>
> —Dale Carnegie

Body Language

Topic objective is to learn to use body language effectively.

Okay, so now the nerves are under control ... let us begin by examining if the body sport is also within control. *Body sport* refers to the non-verbal signals emitted through signs that the body makes which to the discerning and critical eye can communicate much more than words. I like referring to it as body sport because it is a game that the body plays without knowledge to the self and hence, the reason why it is invariably *involuntary*, one over which you have no control. There are however, certain gestures that can be controlled for a positive and confident look. These gestures cannot be acquired in a day and require constant practice (see Table V.2).

Table V.2: Tips for Displaying Positive Body Sport

- Direct eye contact and smile
- Feet firm on the ground
- Shoulders square
- Few movements of the hand
- Palms facing upwards
- Steady, controlled movements across the room

In the course of the presentation, while it is good to be natural, adoption and avoidance of certain gestures can change the impression of the speaker in the minds of the audience. Let us take a brief look at some of the positive gestures and try and incorporate them in the course of the presentations. Believe me, you will not be able to use them all at one shot. Practice and gradual adoption in daily communication will make these gestures part of your personality. Facing the audience, using these gestures will then not be problematic or difficult and will flow naturally.

Note: **Adopt positive gestures in daily functioning, till you realize they are second nature to you.**

Direct Eye Contact and Smile

Think of the days when you were a child and had been up to some mischief and had inadvertently been caught in the process. While acknowledging the crime, you would not maintain eye contact. You may also remember being reprimanded for not being able to maintain eye contact. The reason for emphasis on direct eye contact then and today is that it is a sign of confidence, honesty, and surety.

Lack of eye contact during a presentation sends an almost similar signal, 'that something has gone amiss', or 'the presenter is not confident'. These and similar other views begin to surface in the minds of the audience. How then does one establish eye contact or for that matter maintain eye contact?

Let's get started. Arrive at the venue 10 or 15 minutes in advance. Note the seating arrangement. The names of the participants have probably already been put up on tent cards. Mentally divide the room into four corners— left, right, left-centre, and right-centre and imagine the seats are occupied. Practice for a few minutes shifting your eye to extreme seating positions in the room.

Finally, the audience has arrived and now begins the ordeal. Begin by looking at one person in the left group directly in the eye, sweep your glance over the rest of the group members and let your eye rest on one member of the left-centre group. Follow this strategy for all four groups in the first round. In the second round, look at another member directly in the eye and keep shifting your eye to other groups. After some time, the audience members may get used to your shifting your head in a particular direction. Change the sequence of looking at the groups. If you started with the left group, begin this time by looking at a group member in the right-centre and move your gaze in the clockwise or anti-clockwise direction. Remember that when you look at group members, your *gaze* must not focus on the forehead or rest below the chin. It must be a direct eye-to-eye contact.

Couple it with an open smile that reaches the eyes—overall impact—huge and unquantifiable. It is difficult to state what the smile should look like for you to bond with the audience. It should be simple and genuine. A smile is a reflection of the state of mind or the heart. It will only look and seem sincere if the individual is sincerely happy with the situation. Try an occasional smile at the audience members in the course of the presentation. Let it not be a broad smile that extends from ear to ear, but a genuine and sincere one with a faint trace at the corners of the mouth.

The fourth commandment for delivering a presentation—*Maintain direct eye contact and smile genuinely for instant bonding with the audience.*

Standing Posture

Have you ever looked at your standing position? Do you slouch, have a hunch? Or do you stand tall and erect? If it is the last nothing can be better. If not, then begin work on correcting the posture.

Have you noticed there is something very strange about the human body? The minute it comes into contact with any object, like table, chair or podium, it automatically leans against the object for support. While in informal chat, it is acceptable to a certain extent, it is absolutely unacceptable in a presentation. Your role as a presenter is to energize the audience and keep them moving at a fast pace with you. If you begin to take support of other objects in the room, don't blame the audience if they also lean back and subsequently tune off!

For a straight and lean posture, balance your weight on both feet, stand erect with shoulders square, and face the audience. How long will a presentation last? Thirty minutes, 45 minutes, or probably an hour? Give it a shot, it is really not all that difficult to balance your weight equally on both feet. Shuffling or moving on the same spot, resting weight on one leg and then shifting it to the other leg, or resting the posterior on the table, while comfortable do not present you as a positive, energetic presenter.

> The fifth commandment for delivering a presentation—
> *Energize the audience by showing your energy and agility.*

Show energy and agility through your posture and movements. This does not mean that you keep moving throughout or remain fixed or glued to one spot. Maintain a balance between the moves and the stationary postures.

Note: Do not slouch or lean against any object in the room.

Movement of the Hands

'Out, out damned spot', said Lady Macbeth as she washed her hands again and again to wash off the guilt of the murder of Duncan, the King. Hands communicated the crime committed not so far behind.

Yes, hands do, not only for Lady Macbeth, but for all of us, communicate a message. Hence, the need to understand the language of the hands. Certain hand movements communicate a negative message. For instance, keeping your arms crossed over the chest, or hands behind the back or in the pocket. While some people may find these positions comfortable or natural, they are best avoided in a presentation. Analysis of these positions indicates that arms crossed over the chest reveal a closed and defensive person; hands behind the back— authoritative; hands in the pocket—secretive or critical.

Interestingly while we have defined these positions of the hand in a very scientific and objective manner, we need to understand that while studying body sport, all gestures of the presenter are to be considered before we arrive at any conclusion. That is, the expression on the face, the look in the eyes, the hand position and movements, and the posture. However, very few members of the audience are able to study body sport in clusters. Their attention is caught by isolated gestures and impressions are formed—this presenter is positive or negative.

To revert to the position of the hands—now that we have negated all the hand positions, we are left with just one—hands by the side. A perfectly acceptable position, though not very comfortable if you are not used to it. If on stage you decide to adopt this position, you will, after a short while feel that the hands from the sockets will fall off! Practice, and achieve the target.

Use your hands sparingly—use them to emphasize a point. Every time you use your hands, ensure that the palms face upwards. Using palms facing downwards is not viewed positively. It is indicative of an overbearing person with the desire to suppress or subdue. Finally, do not point fingers at anyone in the audience. If you must use your hands to point to any one, use the full palm with all fingers pointing at the respondent. The palm in this case must again be facing upwards.

Warning! Watch out! Do not clench your hands into fists, which would be indicative of the fact that you are not very happy about the topic you are discussing.

Movements of the Presenter

Can you actually remain glued to a point and deliver your presentation? No, don't even try that! You will look and feel like a robot, stiff, unrealistic and unnatural. The audience would like to see you look and behave normal.

For movement of any kind, you must have done sufficient research on the layout in the room. You must be familiar with the extent to which you can move left or right while remaining in the vision of the audience. Additionally, you must also have information on the chords and the wires in the room. Check if the wires of the audio visual equipment are taped to the ground. Check on the seating arrangement. If it is a U-shaped seating arrangement, your life has been made simple by the organizers. If it is in a classroom style with seats arranged in rows, try and get the arrangement changed. Now, you are comfortable with the arrangement and know how and where to move.

Just a Minute: **Have you studied the layout of the room?**

The projector may be fixed in the centre of the room. Begin the presentation by standing on the left side of the U-shape, welcoming the audience, and introducing yourself. After some time you may feel the need to move to the right side, take confident steps and move to the right, without blocking the projector or coming in between the projector and the screen. You can also move to the centre of the U-shape. When you want to move out of the centre of the U-shape, move in reverse gear. The initial research on the layout of the room will at this stage hold you in good stead. You can comfortably move around without knocking into anything or anyone.

Warning! **Exercise caution! Do not turn your back to the audience.**

Positive body language for a presentation then can be summed up as an aggregate of *direct eye contact, feet firm on the ground, shoulders square,* and few *hand movements* with palms facing upwards. A pleasant expression on the face with an occasional smile during a presentation is also essential because it indicates that you are happy to be with the audience.

The sixth commandment for delivering a presentation—
Listen carefully to the questions, rephrase and then give a response.

Voice Modulations

Topic objective is to exercise control over voice inflections.

Sit back and reflect—who according to you is a good presenter? And why? What are the outstanding qualities that the presenter possesses? One of your many responses is sure to be the voice modulations and the inflections that the presenter brings to the floor. Isn't that what media anchors use for various progammes—the quality of voice, the modulations and inflections, the tone, the emphasis, the pauses at appropriate junctures? Think of the radio programmes, in which you are not able to see the presenter, yet you remain tuned on to the system and the programme because of something inherent in both the content and the tone.

This analysis brings us to an interesting point—the need for voice modulations. Remember, the best of presentations and ideas in terms of content can put the audience to sleep if the voice is slow-paced and monotonous. The four components that enhance voice quality and aid in voice modulations are—energy, pace, pauses, and emphasis (see Table V.3).

Table V.3: Enhancing Voice Modulations

1.	Energy	Vary your voice modulations between high, middle and low energy level.
2.	Pace	Vary the pace of speaking.
3.	Pauses	Incorporate pauses at appropriate places.
4.	Emphasis	Emphasize points that you want the audience to retain.

The seventh commandment for delivering a presentation—*Use voice modulations to capture the attention of the audience.*

Energy

Energy in voice refers to the force that a presenter uses to present ideas. Audience members prefer to listen to an individual who has force and energy in the voice than one who makes a presentation in a flat voice, that is, without any voice inflections. There are three levels of energy: high, medium, and low.

Do not begin with high energy, if you are not used to it. It will be difficult for you to maintain and sustain the same level for the rest of your presentation. Begin at the middle level, shoot up to the high energy level, and then come down to the low energy level. It is not necessary to follow this pattern. You can follow any pattern, that is, alternate between the different energy levels. The variations in the energy level help sustain audience interest.

Note: Vary the energy level for maximum gain.

Pace

Do you speak fast or are you very slow? Are the listeners able to grasp what you are talking about or do they tune off? You have to gauge the level of acceptance of your presentation from the facial expressions of the audience. If they have a puzzled look on their face, it indicates that they have not understood a word of what you have said. Vary the pace of speaking. There are individual variations on how many words are pronounced per minute. The important criterion for measuring success is that the audience members are able to understand all that is being said and are able to enjoy it.

A good way to control pace in the practice stage, is to record your speech on the audio system, and then to replay it. This will help you to pick out weaknesses, if any, in the energy and pace of speaking.

> **Just a Minute: Are you able to match the pace of your speaking with the needs of the audience?**

Pauses

Directly related to the pace of speaking is the use of pauses and emphases. Do you pause in the course of a presentation? Do you lay emphasis on the right words?

> The eighth commandment for delivering a presentation—*Weave in the pauses in your presentation and practice thoroughly.*

What is the importance of pauses? Where exactly must one pause? Pauses help the listeners to assimilate what is being said. If you start at a very fast pace and continue at the same pace, it is very difficult for the audience to assimilate the said content. When a point has just been completed, pause for a couple of seconds, look at all the audience members, and try to secure their consent through eye contact. Audience members need time to absorb the points before they begin to concentrate on the next point.

Example

> *In a persuasive presentation for selling computer hardware to corporate houses, if you pause after presenting the financials, the audience members get time to assess the feasibility of the proposal based on financial implications before they yield to further discussion.*
>
> *Don't make haste! Revel in the pause! You have almost won the audience over to your side.*

The second pause can be structured for presentation immediately after presenting the benefits.

Pauses are not only used after points but can also be used after statements or words for dramatic effect.

Example

In a scenario description for the opening of a presentation, you are discussing the impact of the terrorist attacks on the World Trade Center. After making the statement, 'Suddenly the planes crashed into the towers.' You pause ... the audience begins to visualize the scene.

Pauses cannot be too long or too short. If they are too long, the audience may lose rhythm and get restless. If too short, the purpose is defeated. Again, it is difficult to state that 10 seconds is just right or too much and nine just right. When you face the audience and see them leaning towards you, absorbing and assimilating the content in the pauses, you know that you have been able to hit the mark. If you see the audience getting restless, it is a negative sign. You have not been convincing and effective in the use of pauses. Pauses also help determine the pace of speaking.

Emphasis

Closely related to pauses is the technique of using emphasis on words. Emphasize select words in the presentation. The words that carry maximum weight must be emphasized. As a presenter, you are the best judge of the text that you will like the audience to concentrate on. However, at the outset, one can say that numbers and statistics capture the attention of the audience and need to be emphasized.

Example

In a presentation on support service provided by your organization to people and companies across the world, you can make a statement to the following extent: 'Ten thousand people in the last two years have benefited from our organization.'

Emphasize 'ten thousand' and 'last two years'.

Note: Use numbers, they always capture the attention of the audience.

Observing these voice modulations—variation in energy level, shift in pace, pauses, and emphasis can bring about the desired effect in the voice modulations. Some presenters are faced with the problem of bringing about variations in the energy level or tone. Two strategies can be followed:

— reading plays and
— practicing using the voice at different levels .

While reading plays take on the roles of all the characters and read the play aloud with sufficient voice modulations, as if you were part of the group enacting the play. Tape your voice, replay, and listen to the voice inflections. Initially the voice may sound flat, but gradually as you keep practicing, you will find that you have been able to adopt the roles and are effectively delivering the dialogues (see Table V.4).

> *I am a great believer in luck and find the harder I work the more I have of it.*
>
> —Stephen B. Leacock

Note: Check voice for energy level, pace, pause, and emphasis.

Table V.4: Tips for Improving Voice Modulations

Practicing at different levels can be done in the following manner:

1. Pick up any sentence, for instance, 'I need to improve my voice inflections'.
2. Speak this sentence at the lowest possible pitch.
3. Repeat the sentence at different levels of pitch increasing by one level at every repetition.
4. Identify the most convenient band of levels for yourself. Ideally the band should comprise five levels.
5. Practice within this band with different sentences.

Exercising Control Over the Audience

Topic objective is to identify strategies to exercise control over the audience when delivering a presentation.

You have done your audience analysis and are now ready with your presentation. All you need to do is exercise control over the audience and keep them tuned to what you are saying. Remember the audience is not bad. It wants you to succeed, but then you too must provide it with the needed input.

Follow the '2 A' approach for success with the audience.

Adapt the message, that is, translate the message into a language that caters to the needs of the audience and is easily understood by them. For example, if the audience is interested in a presentation on installation and maintenance costs of an X-ray machine, and you provide them with spatial information on the machine, the purpose of the presentation is defeated.

or

If the audience has expressed an explicit desire to gain information from you on the appraisal of the employees in the accounts section and you begin talking to them about the targets of the accounts section, the purpose is not achieved. Speak, as far as possible, the language of the listeners.

Address the message, that is, use pronouns like 'you' or 'your' to refer to the audience.

Example

'*You must have read in the newspapers today...*'

The 'you' reference, as in this particular example, makes the audience alert to the statements made by the presenter.

Another strategy for bonding can be to address the audience members directly by name. The bonding is almost immediate.

> *Before speaking, consider the interpretation of your words as well as their intent.*
>
> —Andrew Alden

Example

'*Mr Mehta, in your capacity as . . .* ' *By addressing messages directly to the audience you draw the attention not only of the addressed individual, but all members in the group.*

Just a Minute: Have you been able to adapt the message to the needs of the audience?.

Audience Interventions

Here is some positive news for you! Audience interventions are a sign of audience interest in the presentation. Your success can, to a great extent, be defined by the nature of audience interventions which are indicative of the fact that the audience has actually been listening to you. If it had tuned off, chances of there being any interventions would not have been possible.

> The ninth commandment for delivering a presentation—
> *Welcome audience interventions ...they help in boosting your morale and building on the presentation.*

Interventions can be in the nature of :

— Agreements
— Additions
— Objections
— Disruptions

Agreements

Agreements are statements made by the audience members through which they indicate their acceptance of a point made by the presenter.

Example

> *In a presentation on the final draft of a project for the electrical department of an engineering college, the faculty member nods and says, 'True, absolutely true.' Or, thanks 'I totally agree with you'.*

Every time there is an audience intervention you must respond to it. Thank the person and then proceed.

Additions

Additions are strategies used by the audience to indicate acceptance of the presenter's point and follow-up with an additional point or anecdote.

Example:

In continuation with the previous example, the faculty member adds an incident and states, thanks 'I totally agree with you. Once in 2001, we had applied a similar process . . . .'

In both these cases, that is, agreements and additions, the presenter must ideally thank the audience member for the contributions made to enrich the session.

Objections

Problems arise when there are objections or disruptions from the audience and the presenter fails to exercise control over the audience. Objections are statements that indicate lack of conformity to or acceptance of statements made by the presenter. The audience member makes an objection, which may be followed by other members. To exercise control, you have to gently agree to disagree and resolve the issue in a peaceful manner.

Example

You are a member of the team of technical support staff in an automobile company. In a presentation on axles, you begin by explaining the merit of the right axle over the left. However, one audience member objects to your statement and says that both the axles are equally important. You can respond in the following manner without offending the audience member: 'Thank you for your observation and comment. If I understand you rightly, in your assertion you would like to state that both the axles are equally important (wait for the audience member to acknowledge the state-

ment. It can be in the form of a loud yes or a nod of the head. Then proceed...) However, recently we found in a study done on approximately 100 cars that the right axle is more important than the left. I will proceed to explain how. In case you have further questions, we can consider them at the end of the presentation.'

The strategy followed in this case was:

- Acknowledgement of the point
- Presentation of further details, and
- Promise to discuss it at a later stage if required

Disruptions

Disruptions are disturbances in the form of questions that are not always logical or structured and are designed to break the flow of the presentation. In such cases, dismiss the question or disruption, or detour and continue with your presentation.

Example

In continuation with the previous example, the audience member may insist that both axles are equally important and that your study is useless and not based on valid grounds. You can respond to the disruption in the following manner: 'I think there is a difference of opinion in our understanding of the function of the axle. Allow me to proceed further. We will pick up the issue after the presentation.'

The crucial stage in a presentation is the question-answer phase in which the audience members sort out their doubts by asking questions.

Answering Audience Questions

Topic Objectives:

- Identify the two types of questions asked by the audience
- Apply strategies to deal with both types of audience questions

Audience questions are an important step in helping you to establish your credibility. The members of the audience are looking for an appropriate or accurate response from you as you are supposedly the expert of the topic, providing guidelines or analysis.

The four steps in responding to audience questions are:

- Listen
- Affirm
- Discern
- Respond

Carefully worded and well thought out responses, at this stage will help you in establishing your *credibility* as a presenter. Do not be in a rush to answer questions. Listen very carefully to the questions, affirm or acknowledge the questions, try and figure out the worth, value, or merit of the questions, that is, *discern* their importance and finally give an answer. Even if you feel that the questions are worthless and a waste of time, do not say so. Make the audience feel that the question is well thought of and worthy of your time and effort. Do not rush through the process. In your haste to give a response, you may use incorrect wordings which may turn the audience hostile.

You can also, on the board or flip chart, make a column with a heading 'parking lot' in which you place all the questions, views, suggestions or comments that could not be attempted in the course of the presentation. As and when time permits, you can revert to the questions and take them up one at a time. This device is extremely helpful as it assures the audience that their questions will, sooner or later be dealt with by the presenter.

The tenth commandment of delivering a presentation is—*Listen carefully to the questions; rephrase and then provide a response.*

When the audience raises simple queries, there is absolutely no problem. You can look terribly interested before framing a response. The two difficult types of questions that necessitate discussion are:

- Multi-pronged questions
- Questions to which answers are not known

Multi-Pronged Questions

The really tough questions are the abstract or *multi-pronged questions* and the questions to which you do not have an answer. Multi-pronged questions are those in which the audience member asks you to give a response to three or four related issues.

Example:

In a presentation on the hygiene conditions in the hospital by the administrative staff, the doctor may ask you the following question: 'Why aren't the right disinfectants being used? How are patients responding to hygiene conditions in the hospital? When was the complaint made, who was on duty?'

The three issues in this situation are

- Quality of disinfectants
- Response of patients, and
- Attendance of administrative staff

For all multi-pronged questions, paraphrase the question before giving a response. 'If I understand you correctly, you will like to know about the quality of disinfectants, response of patients, and the staff who were on duty?'

If the question is not clear, ask the person to repeat the question. Arrange the questions in the order in which you wish to respond. In case you want to begin your answer with the response of patients, paraphrase it in the following manner: 'If I understand you correctly, you would like to know about the response of patients, the quality of disinfectants, and the staff who were on duty?'

In case you do not wish to reveal the answer, you can give the answer to the first two *queries* and miss out on the third. However, the audience may be very keen to get the response from you and may repeat the question. In such situations, you have no option but to give the answer.

Questions to Which Answers are not Known

It may happen that the audience asks you a question to which you do not have an answer. Accept *human frailty* and acknowledge inability to answer the question at that particular moment. Begin by apologizing and respond in the following manner: 'I'm sorry I do not have an answer to this question but I can get back to you tomorrow.'

Another strategy that can be adopted is to throw the question back at the rest of the audience members in the following manner: 'What do you think is the best possible solution?' In 95 per cent of the cases, you will get an answer from some member of the audience. But this is a very tricky strategy as it may happen that no one in the audience has an answer and you are back to square one. For embarrassing situations of this kind, keep a couple of punch lines up your sleeve. In a situation where the audience does not have an answer to the question, you can say with an apologetic smile, 'All of us are sailing in the same boat.' However, the end result of this punch-laden question-answer session is not very productive. The audience is dissatisfied with your performance and all the effort that you had put in planning, designing, and presenting goes a waste.

Warning: **Be careful of multi-pronged questions or questions to which you do not have an answer.**

Checklist for Delivering a Presentation

Do's	*Don'ts*
Follow MAS	Be unprepared
Practice for improving voice modulations	Speak in a monotonous manner
Stand tall and erect	Shift weight from one leg to the other
Maintain eye contact	Look continuously in one direction
Smile frequently	Give a very broad smile
Use hands for emphasis	Point a finger

(*Contd.*)

Table (*Contd.*)

Do's	Don'ts
Move from one side of the room to the other	Stand fixed to one spot
Breathe deeply to control the nerves	Drink water or anything cold before a presentation
Adapt the message	Use high flying statements
Thank the audience for their suggestions	Refute or argue on stage
Listen carefully to the question	Rush with the response
Paraphrase the question	Throw it back to the audience
Accept human frailty	Show knowledge where there is none

SUMMARY

1. Exercise control over MAS: material, audience and self.
2. Ascertain the objective for making a presentation which can be to inform, persuade, motivate to action, sell, teach or train.
3. Control nerves or nervousness by recognizing feelings of fear, breathing deeply, and doing pep talk.
4. Practice on body language to project a positive self image.
5. Bond with the audience by a gentle smile and direct eye contact.
6. Feel and look relaxed in the course of a presentation.
7. Make your presentation energetic, forceful with varied pace and pitch.

8. Structure your pauses and weave in the emphasis at points where you want the audience to absorb and assimilate.
9. Adapt and address your message to the needs of the audience.
10. Listen, affirm, discern and then respond to the audience queries.
11. Handle audience interjections with care.
12. Be truthful and honest in interaction with the audience.

Chapter VI

Situational Presentation

OBJECTIVES

- ❑ Identify relevant issues
- ❑ Assess the nature of presentation needed for the situation
- ❑ Develop a mental frame for the presentation
- ❑ Apply strategies

After reading the book you may have realized that you may still be hesitant, fidgety, and nervous. You need practice and still more practice to be able to come up to an expected level.

Try the following course of action:

1. Pick up any deviant situation or ask a friend to compose the situation for you.
2. Light a matchstick.
3. Think as the matchstick burns (which will be approximately 15 seconds).

4. Blow-out the matchstick as it begins to singe your finger and thumb.
5. Begin speaking immediately.

The purpose of this exercise is to help you in the process of thinking on your feet. The reason why I ask you to light the matchstick is that more than half your concentration will be on the lit matchstick and you will not be able to plan. Yet, if you are able to speak on the impromptu situations given to you, you have already honed your skills and are on the road to becoming a successful presenter.

Some situations and examples are provided in this chapter which will serve as good points to begin with. Once all these situations have been exhausted, you can devise more and perfect the art of effective speaking.

Examples:

1. *You are travelling by train. Your co-passengers, comprising a family of husband, wife and two kids, have been littering the compartment floor with foodstuff and rubbish. Ask them to refrain from it.*

2. *You are driving on the road on a two-wheeler, when your vehicle is hit by a car trying to overtake you from the left. Though the driver stops, he refuses to pay compensation for the dent in your vehicle's body. Convince him to pay for the damage.*

3. *The bank teller is ready to close the counter though there is still some time to go till closing time. Persuade her to get your cheque encashed before she leaves.*

4. *Your classmate had borrowed your notes for reference, and now seems to have misplaced them. Ask him to return them to you at the earliest, intact.*

5. *A senior colleague is in the habit of interrupting group discussions with personal accounts. Put the message across that such behaviour is not appreciated in teams.*

6. *Your friend and you often dine out together. Both of you get along well; however, lately you have realized that you often end up footing the bill. Broach the subject with her.*

7. *Your manager has asked you to submit a report in one day's time. The data, however, is not available and it would take several days to compile the information. Ask for more time to complete the report.*

8. *You are driving a car on a busy road. The car in front of you gives a sudden break, and your vehicle rams into it, denting the rear fender. Though it is obviously not your fault, the driver of the other vehicle demands that you pay for the damage. Stress your stand and do not give in to his demand.*

9. *The neighbour's dog frequently gets into your garden and pulls out the plants. Talk with your neighbour about it.*

10. *You have booked a ticket through a travel agent for an overnight bus journey. When you board the bus, you find the seat broken. How would you handle the situation?*

11. *Mention to your colleague that you do not like her habit of talking about other people when they are not around.*

12. *You and your colleague often have to work together on projects that require working on the computer. She is not conversant with the software, and refuses to learn. As a result, most of the system's work comes to you. Convey to her that she ought to pick up the required skills.*

13. The new project you have been assigned to requires help from a senior colleague. He is not known to be friendly with newcomers. Approach him for help.

14. A friend had borrowed a large amount of money from you six months ago. Now he seems to have forgotten all about returning it. Raise the issue with him.

15. A new recruit in the organization, you realize a senior colleague has been withholding from you information that you would require to accomplish the assigned tasks. Talk with him about it.

16. You have hosted a party in a renowned restaurant, and the food turns out to be substandard. Talk to the manager about this.

17. A friend has had a death in the family and seems to have withdrawn into herself. Talk with her to move on in life.

18. A pure vegetarian, you find a piece of bone in the vegetable Chow Mein you had ordered at a restaurant. Talk to the manager.

19. A close friend has invited you to a party at his place. However, you have an examination the next day, and will be unable to make it. Explain your position to him.

20. The vegetable vendor at the local market has apparently overcharged you for your regular supply. Talk to him about it.

21. On a hiking trip, ask for a lift from a passing car on the highway.

22. Lodge a complaint with the complaint cell of a local department store, for defective goods.

23. The quality of food in the mess is not up to standard. As the students' mess coordinator, speak with the mess supervisor regarding bringing about improvements.

24. Your colleague has asked you for help with a project she is working on, but you will not be able to help her due to lack of time. Politely explain your stand.

25. There is a party to celebrate the successful completion of a major project by your team. As the team leader, make a short speech on the occasion.

26. Convince your friend to read your favourite book in fiction.

27. Midway through a major project, you need to take two days off for a medical check-up. With the deadline soon approaching, ask your project leader for leave.

28. The tailor has messed up the suit you had ordered. Ask him to alter it, at no extra cost.

29. Visualize yourself at a hill station on a winter morning. Build up an imagery of the environment.

30. You have earned a well-deserved holiday after a lengthy project. Now your senior wants you to carry some routine file work to complete during your vacation. How would you refuse?

31. You are working on your friend's computer, and accidently delete some of her files. Break the news to her.

32. A senior colleague keeps the ring volume of her cell phone very high, even during meetings. Talk to her as to how distracting it is for others in the room.

33. Convince your non-vegetarian friend to turn vegetarian.

34. How would you explain Newton's law of gravity to a six-year old child?

35. While on a long bus journey you find an elderly person smoking constantly. Ask him to stop.

36. You come to hear that one of your colleagues has been discussing about you with other people, while

you are not around. Tell her that you do not like it and she should refrain from it.

37. *Imagine yourself staying in a hostel with very strict rules. You need to stay late for a friend's party. Convince the hostel warden to allow you to stay out beyond the stipulated time.*

38. *A friend often borrows your bike, but returns it without filling the petrol. Refuse to lend it to him the next time he asks for it.*

39. *Your boss wants you to work over the weekend on a project which you know you have not been officially assigned to. Assert yourself, and politely refuse to do the work.*

40. *Your boss has called you for a meeting to discuss a problem in the ongoing project. However, he seems distracted and is apparently not giving you his full attention. Draw his interest back to the issue at hand.*

41. *You have made a terrible mistake for which the company had to incur a heavy loss. The top management is furious and has asked for your resignation. How would you pacify the top management and ask for one more opportunity.*

42. *Your boss is a coercive type of manager who doesn't listen to any ideas at all. You have some ideas, which when implemented, would definitely increase the productivity. How do you convince your boss so that he implements your ideas?*

43. *You are known to be empathetic and a good listener. Most of your time in office is spent in listening to the problems of other people. How would you correct this situation so that you have ample time to concentrate on your job?*

44. *An ambitious project has been assigned to your company. You spring on the opportunity and take full responsibility for it. Later you realize that you*

cannot do full justice to it because of some serious family problem. Your Boss is banking on you to deliver the results and the deadline is fast approaching. How would you communicate your inability to deliver the goods on time?

45. Your boss has given an interview in the newspaper where he has made a complete fool of himself. How do you explain to him that he is in dire need of a proper public relations officer?

46. You have a colleague who has an ego problem. He is not receptive to the ideas of others and tries to impose his viewpoint on the group. You have to persuade him to act not as a team leader but as a team member.

47. You are a project manager in an IT firm. You are meeting with one of your prospective clients. He is demanding for faster completion of project (say eight weeks) but you know it can't be completed before 12 weeks. You have to convince the client and get the project.

48. Convince your superior that the plagiarized report is actually your own work.

49. Motivate a junior employee to put in four hours of extra work without getting paid for it.

50. Your client is terribly annoyed as you were unable to provide the goods at the stipulated time. Defend your company.

Glossary

Presentation A formal mode of orally conveying ideas from the sender to the receiver/s. Formal presentations are largely a public affair where the presenter faces the audience and delivers ideas, mostly as a monologue

Informative presentation A presentation in which an attempt is made to educate or inform the audience members on issues or processes in the organization

Persuasive presentation A presentation in which an attempt is made to sell the idea or make a sales pitch to the audience

Audience expectations What the audience is looking for from the presentation, in terms of information, benefits and value addition

Aids Supplements such as slides, handouts, recordings, or instruments that may be used to support the oral presentation

Cue cards Small thick paper cards, each representing a point from the collated material, used to structure the presentation material in a logical sequence

Anecdote Narration A story-telling technique of beginning a presentation or giving a boost to the sagging presentation

Scenario Description An anecdote narration technique in which the environment and surroundings are also taken into account

Quotations A statement or a bunch of statements made by a renowned personality that help in the development of the case

Declaration A statement made at the opening of a presentation in which a promise is made or a startling statement made that captures the attention of the audience

Statistics The science of collecting and analysing significant numerical data

Visual Imagery A set of words that stimulates the sense of perception of the audience members and helps them to visualize the situation that is being explained

Rehearsal The practice of the presentation material

Body language The non-verbal signals emitted through signs that the body makes

Gaze Look or eye movement

Posture Standing position of the body

Voice modulation The change in stress, pitch, loudness, or tone of the voice; an inflection of the voice

Pace of speech The rate of speaking; number of words per minute

Word emphasis Stress on certain words

Message adaptation Translating the message into a language that caters to audience needs or is easily understood by members of the audience

Multi-pronged question Questions in which two or more related questions are asked

Credibility The worthiness of belief in a concept or product

Queries Questions

Human Frailty Human weakness

Spatial Of space

Thesis Proposition to be maintained and proved

Voice Inflections Variations in voice modulations

Table Representation of specific data

Single line graph Graph with one line used to show growth

Double line graph Comparative graph with two lines that shows growth

Bar chart Bars projected vertically to show quantities

Stacked Bar Chart Vertical bars placed one on top of the other with multiple data

Pictogram Creative and innovative ways of representing and analysing the data in the forms of symbols

Flow chart Shows the relationship between processes, procedures, and concepts

Pie Chart Represents percentage and is plotted in the form of a circle

Floating Wedge Part of the pie chart that is not joined to the circle but sticks out

Organizational Chart A chart that shows hierarchy in an organization

Paraphrase Rephrase

Handouts Hard copy of text

Memory joggers Memory refreshers

Six-by-six rule Six lines with each line containing six words

Incline Rise

Decline Fall

Plateau Even/horizontal

Index

About the Author

Asha Kaul is Associate Professor, Communications Area, Indian Institute of Management, Ahmedabad. She obtained her doctorate from the Indian Institute of Technology, Kanpur, in 1990 and also holds a master's degree in English. Asha Kaul has previously been a communications consultant to several public and private sector organizations. Her current areas of interest include 'genderlect' and gender sensitivity in the corporate world. Dr Kaul has designed and developed workshops and training material in communication and presentation skills for various corporate houses in India. She is the author of *Business Communication* (1998) and *Effective Business Communication* (2000) and has also written numerous articles and book reviews for journals of repute and for websites.